Contents

Dedication

For everyone who's ever been comforted by a cup of Mom's hot cocoa or a dish of macaroni & cheese.

Appreciation

Thanks to all of you who shared your families' most satisfying recipes and heartfelt memories with us!

Comfort Foods

Homestyle recipes for feel-good foods like Mom used to make.

A Country Store In Your Mailbox®

Gooseberry Patch
600 London Road
P.O. Box 190
Delaware, OH 43015

www.gooseberrypatch.com
1·800·854·6673

Copyright 2007, Gooseberry Patch 978-1-933494-39-5
Third Printing, March, 2008

Do you have a tried & true recipe...
tip, craft or memory that you'd like to see featured in a **Gooseberry Patch**
cookbook? Visit our website at **www.gooseberrypatch.com**, register
and follow the easy steps to submit your favorite family recipe.
Or send them to us at:

Gooseberry Patch
Attn: Book Dept.
P.O. Box 190
Delaware, OH 43015

Don't forget to include the number of servings your recipe makes,
plus your name, address, phone number and e-mail address.
If we select your recipe, your name will appear right along
with it...and you'll receive a **FREE** copy of the book!

Breakfast

Yummy, yummy, yummy...sticky buns in my tummy!

Overnight Blueberry French Toast

Gloria Bills
Plymouth, MI

This delicious recipe has become a holiday tradition at our house...my husband and children love it! It's easy to make the night before, then in the morning, just pop it in the oven.

1 baguette loaf, sliced 1-inch
   thick
6 eggs
3 c. milk
1 c. brown sugar, packed
   and divided

vanilla extract to taste
nutmeg to taste
1/4 c. chopped pecans
2 c. blueberries
Optional: maple syrup

Arrange baguette slices in a lightly greased 13"x9" baking pan; set aside. In a large bowl, whisk together eggs, milk, 3/4 cup brown sugar, vanilla and nutmeg. Pour mixture evenly over baguette slices. Cover and chill overnight. Just before baking, sprinkle remaining brown sugar, pecans and blueberries over top. Bake, uncovered, at 350 degrees for 30 minutes, until golden and bubbly. Serve with maple syrup, if desired. Serves 6 to 8.

Get your day off to a sunny start!
Whip up an overnight breakfast dish the
night before and refrigerate it...all ready
to pop in the oven in the morning.

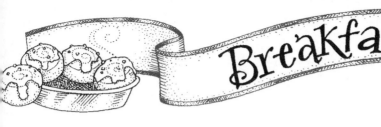

Brown Sugar Baked Oatmeal

Sharon Demers
Dolores, CO

When I was a little girl, Mom would have freshly baked oatmeal raisin cookies ready when I came home from school. This recipe reminds me of them...such a warm & cozy memory.

1/2 c. butter, softened
1/2 c. brown sugar, packed,
   or 1/2 c. honey
2 eggs, beaten
3 c. long-cooking oats,
   uncooked
2 t. baking powder

1 t. salt
1 c. milk
Optional: chopped dried fruit
   or nuts
Garnish: applesauce, honey,
   maple syrup

Blend together butter and brown sugar or honey. Add eggs; mix well. Stir in oats, baking powder, salt, milk and fruit or nuts, if using. Pour into a greased 8"x8" baking pan; bake for 30 minutes at 350 degrees. Serve with applesauce, honey or maple syrup. Makes 4 to 6 servings.

Serve up sweet memories...bring out Grandma's vintage toast rack and jelly dish to use on the breakfast table.

Bacon & Egg Potato Skins

Dale Duncan
Waterloo, IA

A tummy-filling complete meal in a potato skin...yummy!

2 baking potatoes
4 eggs, beaten
1 to 2 t. butter
salt and pepper to taste
1/4 c. shredded Monterey Jack
  cheese

1/4 c. shredded Cheddar
  cheese
4 slices bacon, crisply cooked
  and crumbled
Optional: sour cream, chopped
  fresh chives

Bake potatoes at 400 degrees for one hour, until tender. Slice potatoes in half lengthwise; scoop out centers and reserve for another recipe. Place potato skins on a lightly greased baking sheet. Bake at 400 degrees for 6 to 8 minutes, until crisp. Remove from oven. In a skillet over medium heat, scramble eggs in butter just until they begin to set. Add salt and pepper; remove from heat. Spoon equal amounts of eggs, cheese and bacon over each potato skin. Reduce heat to 350 degrees and bake for 10 minutes, until cheese is melted and eggs are completely set. Garnish with sour cream and chives, if desired. Makes 4 servings.

Stir a spoonful of strawberry jam or orange marmalade into hot tea for extra sweetness.

Breakfast Pie

Sharon Tillman
Hampton, VA

Nothing says "Rise & shine!" on a lazy weekend morning like the heavenly aroma of this pie in the oven.

3 eggs, beaten
1/2 c. milk
1/2 t. salt
pepper to taste
5 T. butter, melted
3 c. frozen shredded
    hashbrowns, thawed

1 c. cooked ham, finely
    chopped
1/2 c. onion, finely chopped
1/2 c. green pepper, chopped
1/4 c. diced pimento, drained
1 c. shredded sharp Cheddar
    cheese

Whisk together eggs, milk, salt and pepper; set aside. Drizzle butter over a 9" pie plate; pat hashbrowns into bottom and up sides to form a crust. Bake at 425 degrees for 25 minutes, or until golden; cool. Sprinkle crust with ham, onion, green pepper, pimento and cheese; top with egg mixture. Reduce heat to 375 degrees; bake for an additional 35 to 40 minutes, until eggs are set. Let stand for 10 minutes before serving. Makes 4 to 6 servings.

Serve up a little whimsy with breakfast! Pour pancake batter into squirt bottles and squeeze the batter directly onto a hot, greased griddle to form hearts, bunnies, cats or your child's favorite animal.

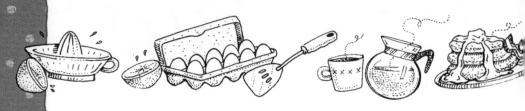

Morning Glory Muffins

Carol Moore
Waynesburg, PA

*With carrots, apple, raisins, pecans and coconut hidden inside,
these yummy muffins are good for you...but don't tell anyone!*

2 c. all-purpose flour
1-1/4 c. sugar
2 t. baking soda
2 t. cinnamon
1/2 t. salt
2 c. carrots, peeled and grated
1 apple, cored, peeled and
  grated
1/2 c. raisins

1/2 c. chopped pecans
1/2 c. sweetened flaked
  coconut
3 eggs
1 c. oil
2 t. vanilla extract
Garnish: powdered sugar,
  cream cheese spread

Mix together flour, sugar, baking soda, cinnamon and salt in
a large bowl. Stir in carrots, apple, raisins, pecans and coconut;
set aside. Blend together eggs, oil and vanilla; stir into flour
mixture. Mix well. Fill 14 paper-lined muffin cups 2/3 full. Bake
at 350 degrees for 20 minutes. Dust with powdered sugar; serve
with cream cheese spread. Makes 14 muffins.

Enjoy a warm muffin anytime! Extra muffins
can be wrapped in aluminum foil and kept in
the freezer for up to a month. To serve, reheat
at 300 degrees for 15 to 18 minutes.

Caramel Apple Muffins

Stephanie White
Idabel, OK

An extra-special breakfast treat.

2 c. all-purpose flour
3/4 c. sugar
2 t. baking powder
1/2 t. salt
2-1/2 t. cinnamon
1 egg, beaten
1 c. milk

1/4 c. butter, melted
1-1/2 t. vanilla extract
1/2 c. apple, cored, peeled
  and finely diced
12 caramels, unwrapped
  and diced

Combine flour, sugar, baking powder, salt and cinnamon in a large bowl; set aside. In a separate large bowl, mix together egg, milk, butter and vanilla; add flour mixture, stirring just until blended. Stir in apples and caramels. Divide batter evenly among 12 greased muffin cups; bake at 350 degrees for 25 minutes, or until tops spring back when lightly pressed. Serve warm. Makes one dozen.

For the tenderest muffins, stir batter just until moistened...a few lumps won't matter.

French Toast

Jeff Reichert
Gooseberry Patch

Delicious topped with warmed strawberry preserves.

4 eggs	4 slices bread
1/4 c. milk	1 to 2 T. butter
1/2 t. vanilla extract	Garnish: maple syrup or
1/4 t. cinnamon	powdered sugar

Whisk together eggs, milk, vanilla and cinnamon in a shallow bowl until well blended. Lay bread slices in mixture; let stand for several minutes until absorbed, turning once. Melt butter on a griddle over medium-high heat. Carefully add bread slices in a single layer. Cook until crusty and golden on bottom, about 2 minutes; turn and cook other side. Drizzle with syrup or sprinkle with powdered sugar, as desired. Makes 4 servings.

Old-Time Milk Toast

Kathy Grashoff
Fort Wayne, IN

Just right when you're feeling a little under the weather.

2 slices bread, toasted	1 t. sugar
2 t. butter, softened	1/8 t. nutmeg
1 c. milk	

Spread toasted bread with butter and place in a shallow bowl. Gently heat milk, sugar and nutmeg in a small saucepan over low heat; stir until sugar dissolves. Pour over toast; let stand until toast swells up and absorbs milk mixture. Serve warm. Serves 2.

Set aside day-old bread for French toast...
it absorbs milk better than bakery-fresh bread.

Finnish Cinnamon Toast

Sherry Saarinen
Hancock, MI

This is a wonderful treat brought over from Finland in 1901 by my great-grandmother. She and my grandmother raised me and taught me to cook some of the old family recipes. This one is an all-time favorite...always delicious on a cold winter morning.

2 envs. active dry yeast
1 c. warm water
2 c. milk
1/2 c. margarine
1 c. sugar, divided
2 t. salt

2 eggs, beaten
9 to 10 c. all-purpose flour
2 T. cinnamon
Garnish: softened butter, hot milk

Dissolve yeast in very warm water, about 110 to 115 degrees. Bring milk, margarine, 1/2 cup sugar and salt just to boiling over medium-low heat; cool. Stir in yeast mixture. Add eggs and 9 cups flour. Knead until smooth and elastic, about 7 to 10 minutes, adding additional flour if sticky; let rise until double in bulk. Form into 6 loaves, about 8 inches long; let rise for one hour. Arrange on greased baking sheets. Bake at 375 degrees for 20 minutes; cool. Slice bread 1/2-inch thick. Mix together remaining sugar and cinnamon; dip each slice into sugar mixture. Return to baking sheet and bake until crisp and golden, turning occasionally. Store in a paper bag. To serve, butter several slices and place in a bowl; top with hot milk. Makes about 8 dozen.

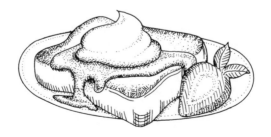

Sprinkle a few drops of hot water on your forearm...
if it doesn't feel too hot or too cold, it's just the right
temperature for dissolving yeast.

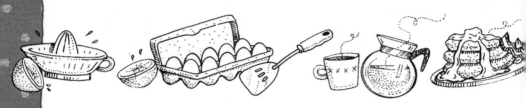

Gingerbread Waffles

Robin Hill
Rochester, NY

Breakfast just doesn't get any better than this!

2 c. all-purpose flour
1 t. baking soda
1 t. baking powder
1 t. ground ginger
1/2 t. cinnamon
1/4 t. ground cloves
2 t. fresh ginger, peeled
  and minced
1/4 t. salt

1/4 t. pepper
2 eggs
1/4 c. sugar
1 c. milk
1/2 c. molasses
6 T. butter, melted
2 T. oil
1 T. lemon juice

Combine first 9 ingredients in a large bowl; mix well and set aside. In a small bowl, whisk together remaining ingredients. Add egg mixture gradually to flour mixture; stir until well blended. Bake until golden in a lightly greased waffle iron, according to manufacturer's instructions. Serve with warm Blueberry-Maple Syrup. Makes one dozen waffles.

Blueberry-Maple Syrup:

1 c. sugar
1 c. water
1/2 t. cinnamon
1 t. lemon zest

2 T. lemon juice
2 c. blueberries
1/4 c. maple syrup
1/8 t. salt

Stir together sugar, water, cinnamon, lemon zest and lemon juice in a saucepan over medium heat; bring to a boil. Reduce heat and simmer, stirring often, for 5 minutes, until thickened slightly. Add berries; simmer for an additional 10 to 15 minutes, until berries pop. Remove from heat; stir in syrup and salt. Makes about 2-1/3 cups.

Good Morning Pumpkin Pancakes
Lela Wingerson
Omaha, NE

Don't wait 'til autumn to enjoy this delicious breakfast treat!

2 c. biscuit baking mix
2 T. brown sugar, packed
2 t. cinnamon
1 t. allspice
12-oz. can evaporated milk

1/2 c. canned pumpkin
2 eggs, beaten
2 t. oil
1 t. vanilla extract

Combine biscuit mix, brown sugar and spices in a large bowl. Add remaining ingredients; beat until smooth. Pour 1/4 to 1/2 cup batter for each pancake onto a greased hot griddle; cook until top surface is bubbly and edges are dry. Turn over; cook until golden. Serve with Pumpkin-Maple Syrup. Makes 12 to 16 pancakes.

Pumpkin-Maple Syrup:

1 c. maple syrup
1-1/4 c. canned pumpkin

1/4 t. cinnamon

Combine all ingredients together in a small saucepan. Mix well and warm through over low heat. Makes about 2 cups.

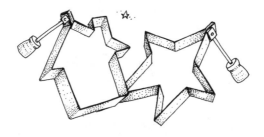

How do you tell when a pancake griddle is hot enough
for the batter? Sprinkle a little water on it...
if it sizzles, the griddle is ready to go.

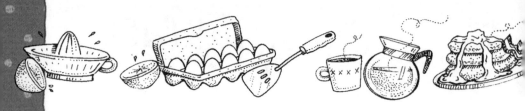

Sausage Brunch Bake

Jill Valentine
Jackson, TN

An oh-so-easy brunch dish that's really tasty.

3 c. herb-flavored croutons
8-oz. pkg. shredded Cheddar
   cheese, divided
1/2 lb. ground pork sausage,
   browned and drained
4 eggs, beaten

2-1/2 c. milk, divided
3/4 t. dry mustard
10-3/4 oz. can cream of
   mushroom soup
32-oz. pkg. frozen shredded
   hashbrowns, thawed

Spread croutons in an aluminum foil-lined 13"x9" baking pan.
Top croutons with 1-1/2 cups cheese and sausage; set aside.
Combine eggs, 2 cups milk and mustard; pour over all. Cover and
refrigerate overnight. Combine soup with remaining milk; pour
over mixture. Spread hashbrowns over top; sprinkle with
remaining cheese. Bake, uncovered, at 325 degrees for one hour.
Serves 8 to 10.

Enjoy fresh blueberries throughout the year...
just freeze them during berry season! Spread ripe
berries in a single layer on a baking sheet and freeze
until solid, then store them in plastic freezer bags.
Later, you can pour out just the amount you need.

Golden Potato Pancakes

Donna West
Spring Creek, NV

A real old-time comfort food, good for either breakfast or dinner.

2 c. mashed potatoes   salt and pepper to taste
1 egg, beaten   oil or bacon drippings for
6 to 8 saltine crackers, crushed   frying

Mix together potatoes, egg and cracker crumbs; add salt and
pepper to taste. Let stand for a few minutes. Heat oil or drippings
in a skillet over medium heat; drop potato mixture by large
spoonfuls into skillet. Cook until golden on one side; flip over
and cook until golden on other side. Makes 4.

Serve Golden Potato Pancakes with chunky-style
applesauce that's warmed and sweetened with a
little brown sugar. Add grilled sausages and a
pot of hot tea for a breakfast that's comforting
on the chilliest morning.

Hot Griddle Cakes

Jennifer Kann
Dayton, OH

Add a cup of fresh blueberries to the batter and serve with bacon or sausage...is there any better way to start the day?

1-1/2 c. all-purpose flour
2-1/2 t. baking powder
3 T. sugar
3/4 t. salt
2 eggs, beaten

1-1/4 c. milk
3 T. butter, melted
oil for frying
Garnish: whipped cream,
    maple syrup

Mix all ingredients except oil and garnish in order given. Drop by 1/4 cupfuls onto a hot, well-greased skillet or griddle. Cook until golden on bottom; turn and cook other side. Serve with a dollop of whipped cream and syrup. Makes one dozen.

Oven Pancake

Britt Wick
Torrance, CA

A hand-me-down recipe from my 95-year-old mother, who first enjoyed it on her farm in Sweden.

2 T. margarine
2 eggs
3-1/4 c. milk
1-1/2 c. plus 2 T. all-purpose
   flour

1 t. salt
Garnish: lingonberry jam,
   whipped cream

Melt margarine in a 13"x9" baking pan. Tilt to cover bottom; set aside. Whisk eggs; add milk, flour and salt, whisking with each addition until smooth. Pour batter into pan; do not stir. Carefully set pan on oven rack; bake at 425 degrees for 40 minutes. Top will puff up and will fall when taken out. Let stand 5 minutes; cut into squares and garnish with jam and whipped cream. Makes 3 to 4 servings.

Soups, Breads & Sandwiches

Nothing soothes the soul like homemade soup and warm bread.

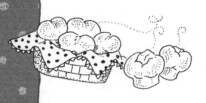  

Homemade Chicken Broth

Doris Stegner
Gooseberry Patch

*A delicious beginning for chicken noodle soup, chicken &
dumplings and oh-so-many other comforting foods.*

3-1/2 lbs. chicken
14 c. water
2 onions, quartered
2 stalks celery with leaves, cut
   into 4-inch pieces
2 carrots, peeled and cut into
   2-inch pieces
2 cloves garlic, halved

2 t. salt
4 sprigs fresh parsley
8 peppercorns
2 bay leaves
2 whole cloves
1/2 t. dried thyme
1/2 t. dried marjoram

Combine chicken pieces and water in a large Dutch oven; bring to
a boil over medium-high heat. Reduce heat to a simmer, skimming
as needed. Add remaining ingredients. Simmer, partially covered,
for one hour. Remove chicken with a slotted spoon. Remove meat
from bones, reserving meat for another recipe. Return bones to
broth; continue simmering for 1-1/2 hours. Line a colander with
several thicknesses of cheesecloth and strain broth, discarding
solids. Chill broth for several hours; lift fat from surface and
discard. Broth may be kept refrigerated for 2 days or frozen for up
to 6 months. Makes 12 cups.

Chicken backs and wings are excellent for making
delicious broth. Buy them fresh at the butcher's
counter or save up unused ones in the freezer
'til you have enough for a pot of broth.

Grandma's Chicken Noodle Soup

Evelyn Belcher
Monroeton, PA

My daughter gave me this recipe years ago...now it's my favorite!

16-oz. pkg. thin egg noodles,
   uncooked
1 t. oil
12 c. chicken broth
1-1/2 T. salt
1 t. poultry seasoning
1 c. celery, chopped

1 c. onion, chopped
Optional: 1 c. carrot, peeled
   and chopped
1/3 c. cornstarch
1/4 c. cold water
4 c. cooked chicken, diced

Bring a large pot of water to a boil over medium-high heat; add noodles and oil. Cook according to package directions; drain and set aside. Combine broth, salt and poultry seasoning in another large pot; bring to a boil over medium heat. Stir in vegetables; reduce heat, cover and simmer for 15 minutes. Combine cornstarch with cold water in a small bowl; gradually add to soup, stirring constantly. Stir in chicken and noodles; heat through, about 5 to 10 minutes. Serves 8.

A pot of chicken soup and a cheery bouquet
of posies are sure pick-me-ups for a friend
who is feeling under the weather.

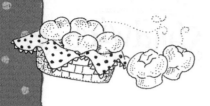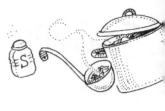

Marie's Vegetable Soup

Marie Needham
Columbus, OH

My mother gave me this recipe many years ago.
The "secret ingredient" is the cabbage...I think vegetable
soup without cabbage is just missing something!

3 to 3-1/2 lb. beef chuck roast
1 head cabbage, quartered
2 onions, chopped
46-oz. can tomato juice
4 15-oz. cans mixed
   vegetables

28-oz. can diced tomatoes
6-oz. can tomato paste
salt and pepper to taste
Optional: favorite herbs,
   hot pepper sauce to taste

Place roast in an ungreased large roasting pan; cover. Bake at 325 degrees for 1-1/2 hours, until half done. Add cabbage and onions to pan; add water to cover. Bake an additional one to 1-1/2 hours, until roast is very tender. Transfer contents of roasting pan to a large soup pot; stir in remaining ingredients except hot sauce. Simmer over medium-low heat for one to 1-1/2 hours. At serving time, break up any large pieces of roast; add pepper sauce, if desired. Makes about 10 servings.

Stir some alphabet pasta into a pot of vegetable
soup...you'll feel like a kid again!

Chicken Pot Pie Soup

Dawn Menard
Seekonk, MA

*My husband works outdoors even in the winter.
There's nothing he likes better at the end of the
day than a nice hot soup with dumplings!*

2 c. cooked chicken, cut into
  bite-size pieces
16-oz. pkg. frozen vegetables,
  thawed
10-3/4 oz. can cream of
  potato soup

10-3/4 oz. can cream of
  chicken soup
2-1/4 c. milk

Combine all ingredients in a large saucepan. Bring to a boil over medium heat; reduce heat to a simmer. Drop dumplings into soup by 1/4 cupfuls. Cook, uncovered, for 10 minutes; cover and cook for an additional 10 minutes. Serves 4 to 6.

Dumplings:

2 c. biscuit baking mix   2/3 c. milk

Stir together baking mix and milk just until moistened.

Pick up a roast chicken or two from the deli...
a quick start for recipes calling for cooked chicken.

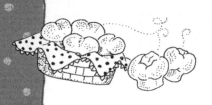

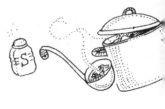

Baked Potato Soup

*Joan Rickert
Poquoson, VA*

*This soup is a real comfort food...warms you up and gives you
a happy tummy! I get requests for the recipe all the time.*

4 to 6 baking potatoes
2/3 c. butter
2/3 c. all-purpose flour
6 c. milk
3/4 t. salt
1/2 t. pepper
1/4 c. green onion, chopped
  and divided

12 slices bacon, crisply
  cooked, crumbled and
  divided
1-1/4 c. shredded Cheddar
  cheese, divided
8-oz. container sour cream

Bake potatoes at 400 degrees for one hour, until tender. Cut
potatoes lengthwise; scoop out pulp and set aside. Melt butter
in a large pot over low heat. Add flour, stirring constantly
until smooth, about one minute. Gradually add milk, stirring
constantly until thick and bubbly. Stir in potato pulp, salt,
pepper, 2 tablespoons green onion, 1/2 cup bacon and one cup
cheese. Cook until heated through, about 5 minutes. Stir in sour
cream. Garnish with remaining green onion, bacon and cheese.
Serves 6 to 8.

When preparing soups that contain dairy products,
easy does it! Cook them slowly over low heat...high
heat causes milk and cream to curdle and separate.

Slow-Cooker Potato Soup

Roberta Simpkins
Mentor on the Lake, OH

Garnish with a sprinkle of snipped fresh chives.

6 potatoes, peeled and cubed
2 onions, chopped
1 carrot, sliced
1 stalk celery, sliced
4 cubes chicken bouillon
1 T. dried parsley

5 c. water
1/4 t. pepper
1 T. salt
1/3 c. butter, melted
12-oz. can evaporated milk

Combine all ingredients except milk in a slow cooker. Cover and cook on high setting for 3 to 4 hours, or on low setting for 10 to 12 hours. Stir in milk during last hour of cooking. Serves 6.

Seal in the flavor of onions and other soup veggies...simply sauté them in a little oil before adding broth and other ingredients.

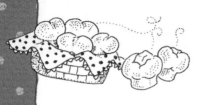

Rainy-Day Tomato Soup

Rosie Sabo
Toledo, OH

Topped with buttery fresh-baked croutons,
this tomato soup is anything but ordinary.

2 T. olive oil
1 onion, thinly sliced
3 to 4 T. garlic, chopped
1 c. celery, chopped
1/2 c. carrot, peeled and cut in
    2-inch sticks

2 c. crushed tomatoes
2-1/2 c. vegetable broth
2 t. dried basil
1 t. dried thyme

Heat oil in a Dutch oven over medium heat; add onion and garlic and sauté until onion is translucent. Add celery and carrot; cook for an additional 5 minutes. Add remaining ingredients and bring to a boil. Reduce heat; cover and simmer for 1-1/2 hours, or until thickened. Place croutons in 4 soup bowls and ladle soup over top. Serves 4.

Croutons:

1 loaf day-old bread, crusts
    removed, cubed

1/2 c. butter, melted
favorite seasonings to taste

Place bread cubes in a large plastic zipping bag; set aside. Combine butter and seasonings; pour over bread. Mix well; arrange on an ungreased baking sheet. Bake at 350 degrees for 10 minutes; turn over and bake for an additional 5 minutes.

Nothing perks up the flavor of tomato soup like fresh basil! Keep a pot of basil in the kitchen windowsill and just pinch off a few leaves whenever they're needed.

Heavenly Hot Ham & Cheese

Amy Jones
Buckhannon, WV

This yummy recipe is from my grandmother.

1 lb. very thinly sliced deli ham
1/2 lb. American cheese, diced
1/3 c. mayonnaise
1/3 c. brown mustard

1/3 c. sweet pickle relish
1 onion, finely chopped
4 hamburger buns, split

Combine all ingredients except buns; spoon onto buns. Wrap individually in aluminum foil; bake at 350 degrees for 20 minutes. Serves 4.

Lighten up your old favorite, grilled cheese...
spritz the bread with a little butter-flavored
non-stick vegetable spray before grilling,
instead of spreading with butter. You'll
enjoy all the flavor without the calories.

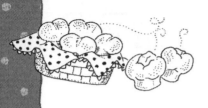

Biffiny's Baked Chili

Biffiny Boozer
Fredericktown, OH

*This chili is perfect for a chilly day, but I
get requests to make it year 'round!*

1-1/2 lbs. ground beef
1 onion, chopped
46-oz. can tomato juice
10-3/4 oz. can tomato soup
2 16-oz. cans dark red kidney
   beans, drained and rinsed

1 c. long-cooking rice,
   uncooked
2 T. chili powder
2 t. sugar
salt and pepper to taste

Brown ground beef and onion over medium heat in a skillet; drain.
Combine with remaining ingredients in a large oven-safe pot; stir
well. Cover and bake at 350 degrees for 2 to 3 hours, stirring
every 30 minutes. Serves 8 to 10.

Mother's Flourbread

Judy Jones
Chinquapin, NC

*My mother used to make this when she didn't have time to
shape biscuits. Splitting a slice open and topping it with
spoonfuls of her homecooked apples was a special treat.*

3/4 c. self-rising flour
1 t. powdered sugar

2 T. shortening
1/3 c. buttermilk

Combine flour and powdered sugar; cut in shortening with a fork.
Stir in buttermilk until it forms into a ball. If dough is sticky,
sprinkle with flour until it's not sticky. Pat out 1/2-inch thick in a
small non-stick skillet. Cook over medium-low until edges are dry
and bottom is golden. Turn over and cook until golden on bottom.
Serves 4.

Soups Breads & Sandwiches

That Yummy Bread

Francie Stutzman
Dayton, OH

Homemade bread with a savory herb filling...mmm!

1 c. milk
2 T. sugar
1/4 c. shortening
2-1/2 t. salt
1 c. water

2 envs. active dry yeast
7 c. all-purpose flour, divided
2 eggs, beaten and divided
1 to 2 T. butter, melted

Heat milk just to boiling; stir in sugar, shortening and salt. Cool to lukewarm and set aside. Heat water to between 110 and 115 degrees; add yeast, stir to dissolve and add to milk mixture. Pour into a large bowl. Add 4 cups flour; stir and beat. Add remaining flour; stir. Let dough rest for 10 minutes; knead on a floured surface until smooth. Place dough in an oiled bowl, turning to coat. Cover and let rise until double. Punch down; shape into 2 balls. Roll each out 1/4-inch thick to a 15-inch by 9-inch wide rectangle. Brush with 2 tablespoons egg, reserving remainder for filling. Spread filling to one inch from edges; roll up jelly-roll style, starting on long edge. Pinch edges to seal; place in 2 greased 9"x5" loaf pans, seam-side down. Brush with butter; cover and let rise for one hour. Slash tops of loaves; bake at 400 degrees for one hour. Let cool before slicing. Makes 2 loaves.

Filling:

2 c. fresh parsley, chopped
2 c. green onions, chopped
1 clove garlic, minced
2 T. butter

3/4 t. salt
pepper and hot pepper sauce
to taste

Sauté parsley, onions and garlic in butter; cool slightly and add reserved egg from main recipe. Add salt, pepper and hot sauce.

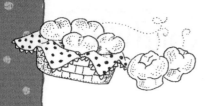

Creamy Split Pea Soup

Kathy Schroeder
Vermilion, OH

*This soup was a favorite at my daughter's recent baby
shower...it will become your favorite too!*

1 lb. bacon, diced, crisply
   cooked and 2 to 3 T.
   drippings reserved
1 onion, diced
2 stalks celery, diced
8 c. water
16-oz. pkg. dried split peas

2 potatoes, peeled and diced
2 t. salt
1/4 t. pepper
3 cubes beef bouillon
1 bay leaf
1 c. half-and-half

Heat reserved bacon drippings in a large soup pot; sauté onion and
celery over medium heat until tender. Add remaining ingredients
except half-and-half; bring to a boil over medium-high heat.
Reduce heat to low; cover and simmer for 45 minutes, until peas
are very tender. Discard bay leaf. Fill a blender 3/4 full with soup;
blend to purée. Return to soup pot; stir in half-and-half. Simmer
over medium heat for 5 minutes, until heated through. Serve with
reserved bacon on top. Serves 8.

Beautiful soup, so rich and green,
Waiting in a hot tureen!

-Lewis Carroll

Chicken Corn Chowder

Cindy Spaziani
Watertown, NY

Everyone at our school luncheons always requests the recipe when they find out how quick and simple this chowder is to make.

2 T. butter
2 boneless, skinless chicken
   breasts, diced
2 onions, chopped
2 stalks celery, sliced
16-oz. pkg. baby carrots, halved
4 c. frozen corn, thawed

4 10-3/4 oz. cans cream of
   potato soup
3 c. chicken broth
1 t. dill weed
1 c. half-and-half
Optional: croutons, additional
   dill weed

Melt butter in a skillet over medium heat; cook chicken until golden. Combine chicken and remaining ingredients except half-and-half and garnish in a slow cooker. Cover and cook on high setting for 4 hours, until carrots are tender. Turn slow cooker off; stir in half-and-half. Let stand for 5 to 10 minutes, until warmed through. Garnish with croutons and a sprinkle of dill weed, if desired. Serves 8 to 10.

Add mild-flavored fresh herbs like marjoram and parsley to soups and stews near the end of cooking time...they won't lose their delicate flavor.

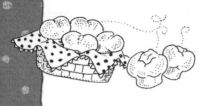

Sloppy Joes

Lori Palmer
East Alton, IL

*I always at least double this recipe...
it's a family favorite and a company pleaser!*

1-1/2 lbs. ground beef
1/2 c. onion, chopped
2 cloves garlic, minced
3/4 c. catsup
1/2 c. water
1 to 2 T. brown sugar, packed

2 T. mustard
2 T. vinegar
2 T. Worcestershire sauce
1-1/2 t. chili powder
8 hamburger buns, split
  and toasted

Cook ground beef, onion and garlic in a skillet over medium
heat until browned; drain. Combine remaining ingredients except
buns in a slow cooker; mix well. Stir in ground beef mixture.
Cover and cook on low setting for 6 to 8 hours, or on high setting
for 3 to 4 hours. Spoon onto toasted buns. Makes 8 servings.

Toast hamburger buns or sandwich rolls before
spooning on juicy fillings...buns won't get soggy!

48

Philly Cheesesteak Sandwiches

Amy Michalik
Norwalk, IA

A hearty meal-on-a-bun.

2 T. butter
1 lb. beef top or ribeye steak,
    thinly sliced
seasoned salt and pepper
    to taste
1 onion, chopped
1 clove garlic, chopped

Optional: 1 c. sliced
    mushrooms
1 green pepper, chopped
1 lb. provolone, Gouda or
    Swiss cheese, sliced
6 hoagie buns or baguettes,
    split

Melt butter in a skillet over medium heat until slightly browned.
Add steak; sprinkle with seasoned salt and pepper and sauté just
until browned. Add onion, garlic, mushrooms, if using, and green
pepper; stir. Cover and simmer for 5 to 7 minutes, until onion and
pepper have softened slightly. Add additional salt and pepper to
taste. Remove from heat; set aside. Lay 2 to 3 slices cheese in
each bun; top with 2 to 3 tablespoonfuls of steak mixture. Top
with additional cheese, if desired. Wrap each sandwich in
aluminum foil; bake at 350 degrees for 10 to 15 minutes,
until cheese is melted. Makes 6 sandwiches.

For zesty French fries that are anything but boring,
spray frozen fries with non-stick olive oil spray and
sprinkle with your favorite spice blend like Italian,
Cajun or steakhouse seasoning. Spread on
a baking sheet and bake as directed...wow!

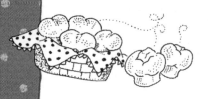

Cheeseburger Soup

Lacy Mayfield
Earth, TX

My son's favorite! When his first-grade class made recipe holders for Mothers' Day, he insisted that I put this recipe in the holder. Kids really do like this soup...the jalapeño doesn't taste hot when it's done.

2 c. potatoes, peeled and cubed
2 carrots, peeled and grated
1 onion, chopped
1 jalapeño pepper, seeded
   and chopped
1 clove garlic, minced
1-1/2 c. water
1 T. beef bouillon granules
1/2 t. salt
1 lb. ground beef, browned
   and drained

2-1/2 c. milk, divided
3 T. all-purpose flour
8-oz. pkg. pasteurized process
   cheese spread, cubed
Optional: 1/4 to 1 t. cayenne
   pepper
Garnish: 1/2 lb. bacon,
   crisply cooked and
   crumbled

Combine vegetables, water, bouillon and salt in a large saucepan; bring to a boil over medium heat. Reduce heat and simmer until potatoes are tender; stir in ground beef and 2 cups milk. Combine flour and remaining milk in a small bowl until smooth; stir gradually into soup. Bring to a boil; cook and stir for 2 minutes, until thick and bubbly. Reduce heat; stir in cheese until melted. Add cayenne pepper, if desired. Top with bacon just before serving. Makes 6 servings.

Pre-warmed soup bowls are a thoughtful touch that's oh-so simple to do. Just place bowls in a 250-degree oven as you put the finishing touches on dinner.

Cheddar Cheese Soup   *Jo Ann*

My family just loves this rich, cheesy soup!

1/4 c. butter
1/4 c. all-purpose flour
2 12-oz. cans evaporated milk
1 c. beer or chicken broth
2 t. Worcestershire sauce
1/2 t. salt
1/2 t. dry mustard
1/4 t. cayenne pepper
8-oz. pkg. shredded sharp
   Cheddar cheese
Garnish: additional shredded
   cheese, sliced green onion

Melt butter in a large saucepan over medium heat. Add flour, stirring constantly until bubbly. Add evaporated milk; bring to a boil over high heat, stirring constantly. Reduce heat; stir in beer or broth, Worcestershire sauce and seasonings. Simmer for 10 minutes; stir in cheese until melted. Garnish as desired. Makes 4 servings.

Add a creamy touch to milk-based soups and gravies...
just substitute evaporated milk. It's easy to keep on
hand since it needs no refrigeration...just keep a
few cans on hand in the pantry.

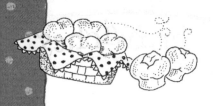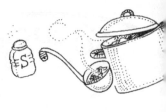

Gooey Buns

Lisa Ludwig
Fort Wayne, IN

Gramps always used an old-fashioned food grinder to grind the bologna and cheese, but you can use a food processor. These tasty sandwiches freeze well.

1 lb. deli bologna, cubed
3/4 lb. pasteurized process
   cheese spread, cubed
1/3 c. mayonnaise-type salad
   dressing

1/4 c. mustard
1/4 c. dried, minced onion
sweet pickle relish to taste
24 hot dog buns, split

Grind bologna and cheese together in a food processor. Add remaining ingredients except buns; mix thoroughly. Spread generously in buns; wrap tightly in aluminum foil. Bake at 325 degrees for 25 minutes. Makes 24 sandwiches.

Grilled Bacon-Tomato Sandwiches

Laura Dossantos
Rutherfordton, NC

Good, quick food that's ready in less than 15 minutes.

8 slices precooked bacon
1 tomato, sliced
4 slices Cheddar or American
   cheese

8 slices wheat bread, divided
1 to 2 T. butter, softened

Layer bacon, tomato and cheese on 4 slices bread; top with remaining bread. Spread outside of sandwiches with butter. Place sandwiches in a non-stick skillet over medium-low heat. Cook for 4 to 6 minutes, or until golden on both sides. Makes 4 sandwiches.

Be creative with everyone's favorite, grilled cheese...
try sourdough, Italian, rye or egg bread
as well as good ol' white bread!

Cheesy Hashbrown Soup

Stephanie Walker
McPherson, KS

This soup is perfect for a cozy winter evening. So quick and yummy, it will soon be a regular on your menu!

1/2 c. green onion, chopped
1/2 c. butter
10-3/4 oz. can cream of
   chicken soup
3 to 4 c. half-and-half or milk

32-oz. pkg. frozen shredded
   hashbrowns, thawed
salt and pepper to taste
1 c. shredded Cheddar cheese
Garnish: chopped fresh parsley

In a Dutch oven over medium heat, sauté onion in butter. Add soup, half-and-half or milk, hashbrowns, salt and pepper. Stir in cheese; heat through. Sprinkle with parsley. Serves 6 to 8.

Keep a bunch of fresh green parsley in the fridge, ready to add a little color and a taste of the garden to meals anytime. Simply place the bunch, stems down, in a glass of water and cover the top loosely with a plastic sandwich bag.

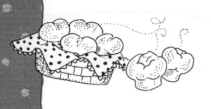

Dan's Broccoli & Cheese Soup

Dan Ferren
Terre Haute, IN

When I was in college, I had an employer that made an out-of-this world broccoli & cheese soup. Now that I'm a stay-at-home dad, I decided to improvise on what I remembered...my whole family loved it! I think it might even be better than the original.

16-oz. pkg. frozen chopped
   broccoli, thawed
10-3/4 oz. cream of
   mushroom soup
1 c. milk
1/2 pt. half-and-half

8-oz. pkg. cream cheese, cubed
6 c. pasteurized process cheese
   spread, cubed
garlic powder and pepper
   to taste

Combine all ingredients in a slow cooker. Cover and cook on high setting for 30 to 40 minutes. Reduce to low setting; cover and cook for an additional 3 to 4 hours, stirring occasionally. Serves 6.

Cream of Broccoli Soup

Belva Conner
Hillsdale, IN

Substitute frozen asparagus for another delicious, easy soup.

10-oz. pkg. frozen chopped
   broccoli
10-1/2 oz. can chicken broth
2-1/2 c. milk
10-3/4 oz. can cream of
   chicken soup

10-3/4 oz. can cream of
   potato soup
Optional: 8-oz. pkg. pasteurized process cheese
   spread, diced

In a large saucepan over medium heat, simmer broccoli in broth until tender. Stir in milk and soups. Reduce heat; heat through without boiling. If desired, add cheese and stir until melted. Makes 4 servings.

Cream of Wild Rice Soup

Lynda Robson
Boston, MA

Spoon into crusty bread bowls...your family will love it!

1/3 c. wild rice, uncooked
1 T. olive oil
7 c. chicken broth, divided
1 onion, chopped
1 stalk celery, minced
1 carrot, peeled and minced

1/2 c. butter
1/2 c. all-purpose flour
2 c. half-and-half
1 t. salt
1/2 t. dried rosemary

Combine rice, oil and 4 cups broth in a large saucepan; bring to a boil over medium heat. Reduce heat; cover and simmer for 30 minutes. Melt butter in a Dutch oven over medium heat; sauté onion, celery and carrot until almost tender. Blend in flour; cook and stir for 2 minutes. Add undrained rice and remaining broth; bring to a boil. Cook until slightly thickened. Stir in half-and-half, salt and rosemary. Reduce heat to low; simmer for 20 minutes, until rice is tender. Makes 8 servings.

Try using fat-free half-and-half in cream soup recipes.
You'll get all the delicious richness without the
calories of regular half-and-half.

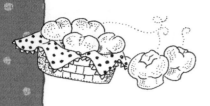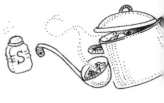

Black Bean Soup

Susan Province
Strawberry Plains, TN

*I love this soup on cold winter days, especially with
a slice of warm, crusty buttered bread.*

6 T. olive oil
2 green peppers, diced
1 onion, finely chopped
1 clove garlic, minced
2 14-1/2 oz. cans chicken
    broth, divided
2 16-oz. cans black beans,
    drained slightly

1 t. Worcestershire sauce
2 T. taco sauce
salt and pepper to taste
Optional: grated Parmesan
    cheese

Heat oil in a soup pot over medium heat. Add peppers and onion;
cook until golden. Add half of one can chicken broth, scraping up
browned bits. Add garlic and cook until vegetables are tender.
Reduce heat; add remaining broth, beans, sauces and pepper.
Simmer for 15 to 20 minutes, until slightly thickened. Add salt
and pepper to taste. Ladle into bowls and sprinkle with Parmesan
cheese, if desired. Serves 4.

A quick & easy way to thicken bean soup...
purée a cup of soup in a blender or even mash it
in a bowl, then stir it back into the soup pot.

Cornbread

Kendra Walker
Hamilton, OH

This recipe was given to me by my mom's good friend, Rita, who's a great cook. It's a must-have at our house with beef stew.

1 c. all-purpose flour
1 c. yellow cornmeal
3/4 t. salt
1/2 c. sugar

4 t. baking powder
1 c. plus 2 T. milk
1 egg
1/4 c. plus 2 t. oil, divided

Combine flour, cornmeal, salt, sugar and baking powder in a large bowl. Stir in milk and egg; beat for one minute. Add 1/4 cup oil and beat for one additional minute. Place remaining oil in an 8"x8" baking pan; tilt pan to coat edges. Spread batter in pan. Bake at 425 degrees for 25 minutes, until golden. Serves 4 to 6.

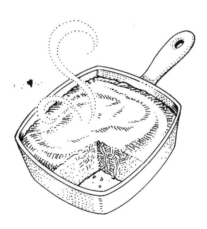

Mom's old cast iron skillet is perfect for baking crisp, delicious cornbread. Before you mix up the batter, drop a tablespoonful of bacon drippings or oil into the skillet and place it in the oven to preheat. When the batter is ready, the skillet will be too.

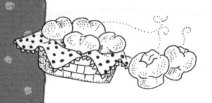

Reuben Soup

Suzanne Ruminski
Johnson City, NY

This yummy soup tastes just like the Reuben sandwich at your favorite deli. Garnish with buttered rye croutons.

5 10-3/4 oz. cans cream of
   celery soup
6 c. milk
28-oz. can sauerkraut, drained

12-oz. can corned beef,
   crumbled
12-oz. pkg. shredded sharp
   Cheddar cheese

Blend soup and milk in a large stockpot over medium-low heat. Stir in remaining ingredients; heat through until cheese melts. Serves 8 to 10.

Polish Sausage Stew

Jean Jensen
Overland Park, KS

A real stick-to-your-ribs meal!

10-3/4 oz. can cream of
   celery soup
1/3 c. brown sugar, packed
27-oz. can sauerkraut, drained
1-1/2 lbs. Polish sausage,
   sliced

4 potatoes, peeled and cubed
1 c. onion, chopped
1 c. shredded Monterey Jack
   cheese

Combine all ingredients except cheese in a slow cooker. Cover and cook on low setting for 8 hours, or on high setting for 4 hours. Skim off any excess fat; stir in cheese until melted. Serves 4.

Scoop out the centers of small round bread loaves for bread bowls in a snap...extra special for serving hot soup or chili.

Quick & Creamy Vegetable Soup

Paula Zsiray
Logan, UT

A tasty comfort food that's easy to make and hits the spot on a chilly day. Use your favorite blend of frozen vegetables.

3/4 c. butter, softened
3/4 c. all-purpose flour
2 c. half-and-half, warmed
6 c. vegetable or chicken broth,
    warmed and divided

2 to 3 c. frozen mixed
    vegetables, thawed
Garnish: dried parsley

Combine butter and flour in a large saucepan over medium heat. Add half-and-half; stir until smooth and slightly thickened. Stir in 2 cups broth. Cook over low heat until blended and heated through, about 4 minutes. Add remaining broth and vegetables. Heat through without boiling until vegetables are tender. Ladle into bowls; sprinkle with parsley. Serves 6 to 8.

Enjoy almost-instant herbed butter tonight!
Press a mixture of dried oregano, thyme,
rosemary and a dash of garlic powder
over a stick of chilled butter and slice.

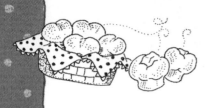

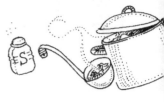

BBQ Beef Sandwiches

Tana Adams
Corona, CA

Hearty homestyle brisket sandwiches everyone will love.

3 to 4-lb. beef brisket
1 c. water
1 onion, chopped
1 bay leaf
1/8 t. ground cloves
1 c. catsup

1/2 c. barbecue sauce
1/2 c. brown sugar, packed
juice of 1/2 lemon
1 T. soy sauce
1/2 T. Worcestershire sauce
6 to 8 buns, split and toasted

Place brisket in a slow cooker; add water, onion, bay leaf
and cloves. Cover and cook on high setting for 8 hours, or until
meat is tender. Remove meat and discard contents of slow cooker;
shred meat and return to slow cooker. Mix together remaining
ingredients except buns and stir into meat. Reduce heat to low
setting and heat through. Discard bay leaf; serve on toasted buns.
Makes 6 to 8 servings.

A trusty slow cooker is the secret to serving warm and
comforting dinners even when you're away from home
all day. Most of Mom's old recipes that call for long,
slow simmering or baking can be adapted to
slow-cooker preparation...give it a try!

Slow-Cooked Pulled Pork

Tina Goodpasture
Meadowview, VA

*A southern-style sandwich favorite...enjoy it like we do,
served with coleslaw and dill pickles.*

1 T. oil
3-1/2 to 4-lb. boneless pork
   shoulder roast, netted or tied
10-1/2 oz. can French onion
   soup

1 c. catsup
1/4 c. cider vinegar
2 T. brown sugar, packed
12 sandwich rolls, split

Heat oil in a skillet over medium heat. Add roast and brown on all sides; remove to a slow cooker and set aside. Mix soup, catsup, vinegar and brown sugar; pour over roast. Cover and cook on low setting for 8 to 10 hours, until roast is fork-tender. Remove roast to a platter; discard string and let stand for 10 minutes. Shred roast, using 2 forks; return to slow cooker and stir. Spoon meat and sauce onto rolls. Makes 12 servings.

If soup or stew tastes bland, just drop in a bouillon cube
or two to add savory flavor in a jiffy.

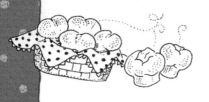

Pasta e Fagioli

Sandra Rocca
Wellington, OH

*My grandmother called this "Dirty Soup"...all of her children,
grandchildren and great-grandchildren still love it! Served
with a fresh, crunchy Italian salad, it's a meal.*

1 onion, diced
2 T. olive oil
3 cloves garlic, diced
15-oz. can crushed tomatoes
5 to 5-1/2 c. water
2 15-1/2 oz. cans Great
   Northern beans, drained
   and rinsed

1 T. dried parsley
salt and pepper to taste
1 T. dried basil
16-oz. pkg. small shell
   macaroni, cooked
Garnish: grated Parmesan
   cheese

In a large pot over medium heat, sauté onion in oil until softened,
stirring constantly. Add garlic; cook until tender, one to 2 minutes.
Stir in tomatoes, water, beans, parsley, salt and pepper. Bring to
a boil; reduce heat and simmer for about 45 minutes. If sauce
thickens too much, add more water. Stir in basil and macaroni;
heat through, about 5 minutes. Ladle into bowls; sprinkle with
Parmesan cheese. Serves 6.

If canned beans don't agree with you, just
drain and rinse them before using...you'll
be washing away any "tinny" taste too.

Italian Bread

Francie Stutzman
Dalton, OH

We love this bread with homemade vegetable soup or spaghetti...it disappears very quickly!

2 envs. active dry yeast
2-1/2 c. water
2 t. salt
1/4 c. olive oil
1/4 c. sugar

7 c. all-purpose flour
1/4 c. cornmeal
1 egg white
1 T. cold water

In a large bowl, dissolve yeast in very warm water, between 110 and 115 degrees. Stir in salt, oil and sugar. Add flour; mix well. Shape into a ball and place in a well-oiled bowl, turning to coat well. Cover and let rise until double in bulk, about one hour. Punch down. Divide into 3 equal parts; shape into loaves. Place loaves crosswise on a greased baking sheet that has been sprinkled with cornmeal. Cover; let rise for 30 minutes. Make 4 diagonal slices in top of each loaf. Bake at 400 degrees for 25 to 30 minutes. Whisk together egg white and cold water; brush onto loaves. Bake for an additional 5 minutes. Makes 3 loaves.

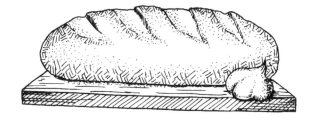

Many's the long night I've dreamed of cheese...
toasted, mostly.

-Robert Louis Stevenson

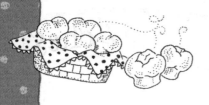

Slow-Cooker 7-Bean Stew

Jodi Mathena
Hereford, PA

*Ladle over steamed rice and serve with cornbread
for a crowd-pleasing soup supper.*

1 lb. ground beef
1 onion, chopped
1 t. garlic, minced
1/2 lb. ground pork sausage
1/2 lb. bacon, chopped
16-oz. can lima or butter
   beans
16-oz. can kidney beans
16-oz. can garbanzo beans
16-oz. can black beans

16-oz. can Great Northern
   beans
16-oz. can pinto beans
16-oz. can pork & beans
3/4 c. brown sugar, packed
1/2 c. catsup
2 T. vinegar
1 T. mustard
1 t. salt

Brown ground beef, onion and garlic together; drain and place in a
slow cooker. Brown sausage and bacon separately. Drain; add to
slow cooker along with all of the undrained beans. Stir together
remaining ingredients; pour into slow cooker and mix together.
Cover and cook on low setting for 8 to 10 hours. Serves 8 to 10.

Stock your freezer with comforting home-cooked
soups and stews, ready to enjoy anytime! They
freeze well for up to 3 months in plastic freezer
containers…just thaw overnight in the refrigerator
and add a little water when reheating.

64

Italian Meatball Soup

Kristen Mitchell
Bartlett, IL

Garnish with freshly shredded Parmesan cheese for extra flavor.

2 T. olive oil
1 red onion, chopped
1 clove garlic, minced
1/2 t. salt
1/2 t. pepper
8 c. chicken broth

20 frozen meatballs
15-1/2 oz. can diced tomatoes
1 c. small shell macaroni,
   uncooked
1/4 c. grated Parmesan cheese

Heat oil over medium heat in a large stockpot. Add onion and garlic; sauté until tender, about 3 minutes. Stir in salt, pepper and broth; bring to a boil. Add meatballs, tomatoes and shells; reduce heat and simmer for 10 minutes, or until shells are tender. Sprinkle with Parmesan cheese. Serves 6.

Homemade butter on freshly baked bread...what a treat!
Pour 1/2 pint of heavy cream into a small jar, close the
lid tightly and shake the jar...let the kids take turns.
Butter starts to form in about 5 minutes and will be
ready in 10 to 15. Drain off the liquid
and add a bit of salt. Yum!

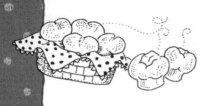

Creamy Tuna Melt

Cindy Atkins
Vancouver, WA

Mmm...how long has it been since you enjoyed a tuna melt?

2 to 3 stalks celery, diced
1 onion, diced
12-oz. can tuna, drained
1/2 c. cottage cheese
1/2 c. mayonnaise

1/4 t. garlic salt
1/8 t. sugar
4 English muffins, split and
  toasted
8 slices American cheese

In a skillet sprayed with non-stick cooking spray, sauté celery and onion until tender. Add tuna, cottage cheese, mayonnaise, garlic salt and sugar to skillet. Mix well, breaking up tuna. Cook over low heat until warmed through, stirring frequently; remove from heat. Place toasted muffins cut-side up on a broiler pan. Spread with tuna mixture and top with cheese slices. Broil until cheese melts; serve immediately. Makes 8 open-face sandwiches.

Making biscuits and there's no biscuit cutter handy?
Try Mom's little trick...just grab a glass tumbler
or the open end of a clean, empty soup can.

Soups Breads & Sandwiches

Country Biscuits Supreme

Gretchen Hickman
Galva, IL

These are terrific with beef stew.

2 c. all-purpose flour
4 t. baking powder
1/2 t. salt
1/2 t. cream of tartar

2 t. sugar
1/2 c. shortening
2/3 c. milk

Sift together dry ingredients. Cut in shortening until mixture resembles coarse crumbs. Add milk; stir just until moistened. Turn dough out onto a lightly floured surface; knead gently for about 30 seconds. Roll out to 1/2-inch thick; cut with a biscuit cutter. Arrange biscuits on an ungreased baking sheet. Bake at 425 degrees for 10 to 12 minutes, until golden. Makes 12 to 15 biscuits.

Bean & Bacon Soup

Kathy Grashoff
Fort Wayne, IN

Use any variety of canned soup beans you like.

1/2 lb. bacon, crisply cooked, crumbled and 3 T. drippings reserved
1 onion, diced
2 carrots, peeled and diced
1 green pepper, chopped

2 cloves garlic, pressed
3 c. water
8-oz. can tomato sauce
2 16-oz. cans kidney beans
hot pepper sauce to taste

Heat reserved drippings in a large skillet over medium heat. Sauté onion, carrots, green pepper and garlic until tender. Add water, tomato sauce and undrained beans. Simmer for 15 to 20 minutes, stirring occasionally, until slightly thickened. Stir in reserved bacon and hot sauce to taste. Makes 6 to 8 servings.

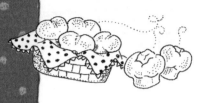

Rachel's Turkey Stew

Rachel Boyd
Defiance, OH

I combined 2 recipes to make this wonderful stew.
Now it's a family favorite...even the kids love it!

28-oz. can turkey, drained and
broth reserved
8-1/2 oz. can corn, drained
and liquid reserved
1-1/2 c. pkg. frozen sliced
carrots, thawed

14-1/2 oz. can chicken broth
1 c. buttermilk
1 T. dill weed
1/4 c. cornstarch

Mix together turkey, corn and carrots in a slow cooker; set aside.
Whisk together reserved turkey broth, chicken broth, reserved
corn liquid, buttermilk and dill weed; pour over turkey mixture.
Cover and cook on low setting for 6 hours. Just before serving,
stir in cornstarch and heat until thickened. Serves 6 to 8.

Pop a simmering stew or soup in a slow cooker and
invite friends to share it with you. Just add a
warm loaf of fresh bread and a pint of your
favorite ice cream for dessert...how cozy!

Best-Ever Vegetable Soup

Betty Burns
Belleville, IL

*Make this hearty soup thicker or thinner as you prefer
by adding more or less noodles.*

2-lb. boneless beef chuck roast
1 onion, chopped
26-oz. can tomato soup
32-oz. pkg. frozen mixed
   vegetables

6 c. medium egg noodles,
   uncooked
salt, pepper and nutmeg
   to taste

Place roast in a one-gallon stockpot; add water to cover. Simmer over medium heat until roast is tender, about 1-1/2 to 2 hours. Remove meat, reserving broth. Trim fat from meat and cut into bite-size pieces; return meat to broth. Add onion and return to simmering; stir in remaining ingredients. Simmer an additional 30 minutes, until vegetables and noodles are tender. Makes 4 to 6 servings.

Homemade soup always tastes even better if made
a day ahead and refrigerated overnight. It's a snap
to skim any fat too...it will solidify on the surface
and can easily be lifted off.

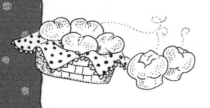

Special Grilled Cheese Sandwich

Lynn Williams
Muncie, IN

Grown-up grilled cheese that's extra rich and delicious.

3-oz. pkg. cream cheese,
   softened
1/2 to 3/4 c. mayonnaise
8-oz. pkg. shredded Colby-Jack
   cheese

3/4 t. garlic powder
1/4 t. salt
8 slices French bread
2 T. butter, softened

Combine all ingredients except bread and butter; blend until smooth. Spread mixture on 4 slices of bread; top with remaining bread. Spread butter on outside of sandwiches. Place sandwiches in a large skillet over medium heat. Grill until golden, about 4 minutes per side. Makes 4 sandwiches.

Hot Dog Chili Sauce

Michelle Campen
Peoria, IL

Everyone loves this homemade topper for hot dogs!
Keep it warm in a slow cooker if you're serving a crowd.

2 lbs. ground beef, browned
   and drained
16-oz. can tomato sauce
6-oz. can tomato paste
3 T. Worcestershire sauce
2 T. sugar
1 T. chili powder

1 T. red wine vinegar
1 t. dried, minced onion
1 t. salt
1/2 t. garlic salt
1/2 t. pepper
1/8 t. ground cloves
2 to 3 drops hot pepper sauce

Mix all ingredients together in a Dutch oven. Simmer over medium-low heat for 20 minutes, stirring occasionally. Serve immediately, or refrigerate and reheat at serving time. Makes about 4 cups.

Sides & Salads

The all-time favorite macaroni & cheese and other delicious sides and salads.

Aunt Annie's Macaroni & Cheese

Elaine Philyaw
Coosada, AL

This recipe was my Great-Aunt Annie's. She was such a sweet and loving person, I know she would want me to share this recipe that has become one of my favorites through the years.

16-oz. pkg. elbow macaroni,
  cooked
1 c. mayonnaise
10-3/4 oz. can cream of
  mushroom soup
4-oz. jar chopped pimentos,
  drained

1/4 c. onion, chopped
1/4 c. green pepper, chopped
1/4 c. butter, softened
16-oz. pkg. shredded Cheddar
  cheese
10 to 12 saltine crackers,
  crushed

Mix together all ingredients except crackers. Spread in a greased 13"x9" baking pan. Sprinkle with cracker crumbs. Bake, uncovered, at 325 degrees for 25 minutes. Serves 8 to 10.

Mom's Macaroni & Cheese

Lecia Stevenson
Timberville, VA

Yummy and oh-so simple to make.

8-oz. pkg. elbow macaroni,
  cooked
8-oz. pkg. shredded sharp
  Cheddar cheese

1 t. salt
1/8 t. pepper
3 T. butter, melted
3 c. evaporated milk

Spread macaroni in a greased 2-1/2 to 3-quart casserole dish. Sprinkle with cheese, salt and pepper; pour melted butter over top. Carefully pour evaporated milk onto casserole. Bake, uncovered, at 350 degrees for one hour. Serves 4 to 6.

Mac & 3 Cheeses

Betty Lou Wright
Hendersonville, TN

Of all the macaroni & cheese recipes I've tried, this is my family's favorite. Don't be shy about adding more cheese!

3 T. butter
2 T. all-purpose flour
1/4 t. salt
2-1/2 c. milk
1 c. Cheddar cheese, cubed

1/2 c. Swiss cheese, cubed
1/2 c. pasteurized process
   cheese spread, cubed
1-1/2 c. elbow macaroni,
   uncooked

Melt butter in a large saucepan over medium heat; blend in flour and salt. Stir in milk; cook until thickened, stirring constantly. Add cheeses; stir until melted. Cook macaroni according to package directions; drain and fold into cheese mixture. Spoon into a lightly greased 1-1/2 quart casserole dish. Bake, uncovered, at 350 degrees for 25 minutes. Serves 8.

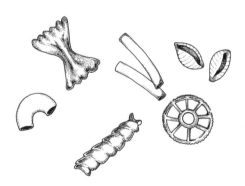

Try using a different shape of pasta next time
you make macaroni & cheese. Wagon wheels,
seashells and bowties all hold cheese sauce well...
they're fun for kids too!

Polly's Mashed Potatoes

Holly Hansen
Joliet, MT

This recipe is requested every time we have a potluck at our church. It is made by a sweet lady, Polly, who's an excellent cook...all the kids absolutely love these potatoes! Polly owned a restaurant for 14 years while raising 8 children and is a sweet grandma who reminds everyone of their own grandmas.

8-oz. pkg. cream cheese,
   softened
1/2 c. butter, softened
1-oz. pkg. buttermilk ranch
   salad dressing mix

5 lbs. potatoes, peeled, cubed
   and cooked
Optional: 2 to 3 T. milk

In a very large bowl, mix together cream cheese, butter and dressing mix with an electric mixer on medium speed. Add potatoes; beat until creamy and fluffy. If potatoes seem too dry, add milk a little at a time. Makes 10 to 12 servings.

For the smoothest mashed potatoes without starchiness,
use an old-fashioned hand-cranked food mill.

Fluffy Mashed Potatoes

Connie Bryant
Topeka, KS

*Try using Yukon Gold potatoes...their yellow color
makes them seem extra buttery.*

6 potatoes, peeled and cubed
1/2 c. warm milk
1/4 c. butter, softened

3/4 t. salt
1/8 t. pepper

Cover potatoes with water in a large saucepan; bring to a boil over
medium heat. Reduce heat; simmer for 20 to 25 minutes. Drain
well; add milk, butter, salt and pepper. Mash until light and fluffy.
Serves 6.

Homemade Gravy Mix in a Jar

Kay Marone
Des Moines, IA

Keep this mix on hand for scrumptious gravy anytime.

2-1/4 oz. jar chicken or beef
   bouillon granules

1-1/2 c. all-purpose flour
3/4 to 1 t. pepper

Combine ingredients; mix well and store in a tightly closed jar.
Attach instructions. Makes 2 cups gravy mix.

Instructions:

To make 2 cups gravy, melt 3 tablespoons butter in a saucepan
over medium heat. Add 1/4 cup gravy mix; cook and stir until
golden, about one minute. Whisk in 1-1/2 cups cold water or
skimmed pan juices until smooth. Bring to a boil; cook and stir
until thickened, about 2 minutes.

Paula's Twice-Baked Potatoes

Paula Smith
Ottawa, IL

*Top with a dollop of sour cream and a sprinkle of
snipped fresh chives...heavenly!*

6 russet baking potatoes
1/4 c. butter
1/2 c. milk
1 onion, finely chopped
6 slices bacon, crisply cooked
   and crumbled

1 t. salt
1/2 t. pepper
1-1/2 c. shredded Cheddar
   cheese, divided

Bake potatoes at 375 degrees for one hour, or until tender. Cool.
Cut a thin slice off the top of each potato and scoop out insides,
leaving a thin shell. Mash potato with butter in a mixing bowl;
blend in milk, onion, bacon, salt, pepper and one cup cheese.
Spoon mixture into potato shells; place on a lightly greased baking
sheet. Bake at 375 degrees for 25 minutes. Top with remaining
cheese; bake an additional 5 minutes, until cheese melts. Makes
6 servings.

Make sure your cutting boards smell fresh and clean...
just rub them with the cut side of a lemon half.

Slow-Cooked Creamy Potatoes

Samantha Starks
Madison, WI

So convenient for potlucks and holiday dinners.

4 green onions, chopped
2 cloves garlic, minced
8 potatoes, sliced and divided
1 t. salt, divided

1/4 t. pepper, divided
8-oz. pkg. cream cheese, diced
  and divided

Combine green onions and garlic in a small bowl; set aside. Layer one-quarter of the potato slices in a greased slow cooker; sprinkle with half of the salt and pepper. Top with one-third each of cream cheese and green onion mixture. Repeat layers twice, ending with potatoes; sprinkle with remaining salt and pepper. Cover and cook on high setting for 3 hours. Stir to blend melted cheese; cover and cook for an additional hour. Stir well and mash slightly before serving. Serves 4 to 6.

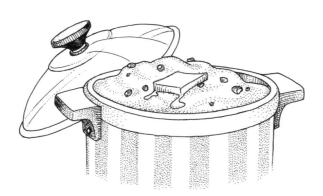

Save any leftover Slow-Cooked Creamy Potatoes
to use in the scrumptious recipe for Golden
Potato Pancakes on page 21.

Scalloped Corn

Judy Voster
Neenah, WI

*My husband loves corn and whenever he's tired after
a hard day on the job, I make this. Add a good movie
after dinner and soon he's feeling much better.*

15-1/4 oz. can corn, drained
14-3/4 oz. can creamed corn
3/4 c. milk
1 egg, beaten
1 c. dry bread crumbs
1/2 c. onion, chopped

3 T. green pepper, chopped
salt and pepper to taste
4 slices bacon, crisply cooked
   and crumbled
2 T. butter, diced

Combine first 3 ingredients; stir in egg. Add remaining ingredients
except bacon and butter; pour into a lightly greased 1-1/2 quart
casserole dish. Sprinkle with bacon; dot with butter. Bake,
uncovered, at 350 degrees for 30 minutes. Serves 4 to 6.

How to know whether to start fresh vegetables cooking
in hot or cold water? Old kitchen wisdom says to
start vegetables that grow above the ground in
boiling water...below the ground, in cold water.

Patty's Broccoli & Swiss Casserole

Donna Esposito
Glenville, NY

This dish is a family favorite that was passed down to me by my late sister Patricia..."Perfect Patty" we liked to call her. Everything she did or made always came out superbly, including this wonderful casserole. It is quick, easy and delicious, and is always expected at our family gatherings. No leftovers here!

1 egg
1/2 c. mayonnaise
10-3/4 oz. can cream of
   mushroom soup
3 10-oz. pkgs. frozen chopped
   broccoli, thawed and drained

1 onion, finely chopped
1 c. shredded Swiss cheese
1/2 c. bread crumbs
2 T. butter, melted
paprika to taste

Whisk egg slightly in a large bowl; blend in mayonnaise and soup. Stir in broccoli, onion and cheese. Pour into a lightly greased 1-1/2 quart casserole dish. Toss together crumbs and butter; top casserole with crumb mixture and sprinkle with paprika. Bake, uncovered, at 350 degrees until bubbly, about 35 minutes. Makes 8 servings.

Flash-frozen vegetables come in so many different varieties.
Stock the freezer with your family's favorites and you'll
always be ready to whip up a delicious side dish
or hearty soup at a moment's notice.

Red Rice

Naomi Cooper
Delaware, OH

Simply delicious with baked chicken or pork chops.

16-oz. can crushed tomatoes
2 T. tomato paste
1 c. long-cooking rice,
   uncooked
1/2 c. water
1-1/2 t. salt

1 t. pepper
6 slices bacon, crisply cooked,
   crumbled and drippings
   reserved
1 c. onion, diced
1/2 c. green pepper, diced

Combine tomatoes, tomato paste, rice, water, salt and pepper in
a medium saucepan; set aside. Heat reserved drippings in a large
skillet over medium heat. Add onion and green pepper; cook for
one minute. Stir vegetables into tomato mixture; cover. Bring to
a boil; reduce heat and simmer for 25 to 35 minutes, until rice is
tender. Stir in crumbled bacon. Serves 6.

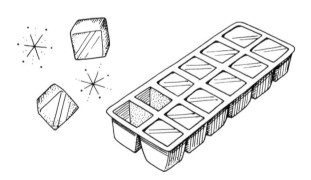

Tomato paste adds rich flavor to casseroles and stews.
Since many recipes only call for a tablespoon or two,
save the rest by spooning it into ice cube trays to freeze.

Beefy Mushroom Rice

Jennie Turner
La Vale, MD

This recipe brings back special memories of my grandma &
grandpa...I used to help them make it when I was growing up.
Now it's a favorite of my own family.

16-oz. pkg. long-cooking rice,
  uncooked
2 10-3/4 oz. cans French onion
  soup
2 10-1/2 oz. cans beef broth
1-1/4 c. water

4-oz. can sliced mushrooms,
  drained
1 c. butter, sliced
Optional: 2 10-3/4 oz. cans
  cream of mushroom soup

Combine rice, French onion soup, broth and water in an ungreased
13"x9" baking pan. Add mushrooms. Arrange butter evenly
over top. Bake, covered, at 325 degrees for about one hour,
until rice is tender. If creamier rice is desired, stir in cream of
mushroom soup; heat through, about 15 to 20 minutes.
Serves 8 to 10.

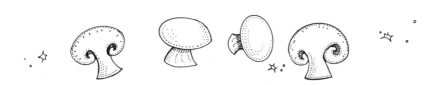

Perfectly cooked rice...as easy as 1-2-3! One cup
long-cooking rice plus 2 cups water equals 3 cups
cooked rice. Stir rice into boiling water, cover and
simmer over low heat for 20 minutes, until water
is absorbed. Leave the pan lid on for a few
minutes more, then fluff with a fork.

Aunt Karen's Baked Beans

Melissa Ward
Ila, GA

These beans have just the right amount of spice. My husband's aunt makes them for all of our family gatherings. I'll pass up dessert to have a second helping of her baked beans!

1/2 lb. ground beef
1/2 c. onion, chopped
2 16-oz. cans baked beans
1/2 to 1 t. garlic, minced
3 T. vinegar
1 T. dry mustard

1/4 c. barbecue sauce
1/2 c. catsup
1/4 c. brown sugar, packed
1/4 c. sugar
3 to 5 slices bacon, partially
   cooked

Brown ground beef and onion together; drain. Combine beef mixture with beans in a large bowl; stir in remaining ingredients except bacon. Pour into a lightly greased 13"x9" baking dish; lay bacon slices on top. Bake, uncovered, at 350 degrees for 55 to 60 minutes, until hot and bubbly. Serves 8 to 10.

Light or dark brown sugar, which should you choose?
Light brown sugar offers mild sweetness, while dark
brown sugar adds richness. Try it in baked beans,
where its distinct molasses taste is especially delicious.

Cinnamon Baked Apples

Karen Pilcher
Burleson, TX

We eat this as a side dish like applesauce, only lots better!

2-1/2 lbs. Golden Delicious
    apples, cored, peeled and
    sliced into 6 to 8 wedges
1/2 c. powdered sugar

1/2 c. sugar
2 T. cinnamon
1/2 c. butter, melted and
    divided

Place apples in a large bowl; set aside. Combine sugars and cinnamon in a small bowl; sprinkle over apples, tossing to coat. Brush a lightly greased 2-quart casserole dish with one tablespoon butter. Add apples; drizzle with remaining butter. Bake, uncovered, at 350 degrees for 30 minutes, or until tender. Serves 6 to 8.

Sprinkle a little fresh lemon juice over sliced apples
before baking...the tart juice will bring out the
flavor of the apples.

Tomato Pudding

Laura Hoevener
Milford, OH

*This recipe came from an old restaurant in Toledo called
the Tally Ho, and was handed down from my grandma.
It's delicious, sweet and savory all at the same time.*

1 c. brown sugar, packed	1 t. salt
10-oz. can tomato purée	4 c. fresh bread cubes
1/4 c. water	1/2 c. butter, melted

Combine brown sugar, tomato purée, water and salt in a small
saucepan. Bring to a boil over medium heat for about 5 minutes.
In a large bowl, toss together bread cubes and melted butter. Stir
in tomato mixture, mixing well. Spread in a lightly greased 2-quart
casserole dish. Bake, covered, at 350 degrees for 45 minutes.
Uncover and bake for an additional 15 minutes. Serves 8 to 10.

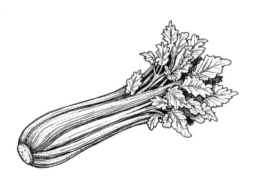

Don't throw away the leaves from fresh celery...
they're full of flavor! Lay them on a paper towel where
they'll dry in just a day or two. Store the dried leaves
in a canning jar to toss into soups, stews and casseroles.

Doretha's Tomato Dumplings

Angie Stone
Argillite, KY

This recipe came from my mother's friend...it has been passed down through her husband's family for years.

1 onion, chopped
6 slices bacon, chopped
1/4 c. margarine
2 28-oz. cans chopped tomatoes

1 c. brown sugar, packed
salt and pepper to taste
12-oz. tube refrigerated
  biscuits, quartered

In a skillet over medium heat, sauté onion and bacon in margarine. Stir in tomatoes, brown sugar, salt and pepper; heat until bubbling. Roll biscuit quarters into balls and drop into tomato mixture, pushing into liquid to coat. Cover and simmer for 15 to 20 minutes, stirring occasionally. Serves 4 to 6.

Why not choose comfort foods as the theme of your next school or church potluck? What fun to see everyone else's idea of comfort...and everything is sure to be scrumptious!

Fresh Southern Tomato Salad

Dawn Van Horn
Columbia, NC

This is one of my favorite salad recipes, so light and full of flavor.
Use home-grown tomatoes, if you're lucky enough to have them!

5 tomatoes, quartered
2 T. olive oil
1 T. red wine vinegar
1 T. fresh basil, chopped

1 clove garlic, minced
salt and pepper to taste
Garnish: seasoned croutons,
   crumbled feta cheese

Place tomatoes in a serving bowl; set aside. Whisk together oil, vinegar and seasonings. Pour over tomatoes, tossing well. Serve chilled or at room temperature, garnished with croutons and cheese. Serves 4.

Special Deviled Eggs

Regina Kostyu
Gooseberry Patch

A "must" at every picnic...these are even better than usual!

1 doz. eggs, hard-boiled
   and peeled
3 to 4 T. bottled coleslaw
   dressing

1/8 to 1/4 t. garlic salt
   with parsley
Optional: paprika

Slice eggs in half lengthwise; scoop yolks into a bowl. Arrange whites on a serving platter; set aside. Mash yolks well with a fork. Stir in dressing to desired consistency and add garlic salt to taste. Spoon into whites. Sprinkle with paprika, if desired; chill. Makes 2 dozen.

Pop unripe tomatoes into a brown paper grocery bag
and store in a dark closet. They'll ripen overnight!

Cabbage Pudding

Teri Johnson
Marion, IN

This is my Grandmother Ellen's recipe from Kentucky. It is always a favorite at carry-ins and everyone wants the recipe.

1 head cabbage, cut into
    1-inch thick wedges
1 sleeve saltine crackers,
    crushed

1/2 c. butter, diced
salt and pepper to taste
1 to 2 c. milk

In a lightly greased 3-quart casserole dish, layer half each of cabbage wedges, crumbs, butter, salt and pepper. Repeat layering, ending with salt and pepper. Pour enough milk over top to just barely cover cabbage. Cover and bake at 350 degrees for 45 minutes; uncover and bake an additional 15 minutes. Serves 8 to 10.

There are so many satisfying ways to fix potatoes!
Whenever you boil potatoes, toss in a few extras
and refrigerate them...you'll have a head
start on your next potato dish.

Stuffing Balls

Jean Kelly
Bruceton Mills, WV

*My mother always made these for Thanksgiving and
Christmas dinners. If you have any left over, they reheat well.*

8 c. soft bread crumbs
2 t. poultry seasoning
2 t. dried sage
2 t. salt
1/2 t. pepper

4 c. celery with leaves,
   chopped
2 onions, chopped
1/2 c. butter
1 c. chicken broth

Toss together bread crumbs and seasonings in a large bowl; set
aside. In a skillet over medium heat, sauté celery and onions in
butter for 5 minutes, until tender. Add broth to skillet. Simmer for
several minutes; pour over crumb mixture and toss to moisten.
Form 1/2 cupfuls into balls and place in a greased 13"x9" baking
pan. Bake, covered, at 350 degrees for about 30 minutes.
Serves 8 to 10.

Day-old bread is fine for stuffing. It keeps its texture
better than very fresh bread...it's thrifty too!

Cornbread-Biscuit Dressing

Jennifer Kann
Dayton, OH

*Bake up your favorite packaged cornbread and
biscuit mixes to make this tasty stuffing.*

4 c. cornbread crumbs
4 c. biscuit crumbs
6 stalks celery, chopped
1 onion, chopped
1/3 c. butter, melted
1 T. dried parsley

1 t. dried sage
1 t. salt
1 t. pepper
2-1/2 c. chicken or turkey
    broth
1/2 c. milk

Spread cornbread and biscuit crumbs on an ungreased baking
sheet. Bake at 300 degrees for 15 minutes, until crumbs are
toasted, stirring twice. Set aside. Sauté celery and onion in butter
over medium heat until tender; remove from heat. In a large bowl,
combine celery and crumb mixtures with seasonings. Stir in broth
and milk; toss to mix. Spoon into a greased 13"x9" baking pan.
Bake, uncovered, at 350 degrees for one hour, or until golden.
Serves 10.

Don't let day-old bread go to waste! Cut it into cubes,
pack into freezer bags and freeze...it's perfect for
making a savory stuffing or herbed salad croutons.

Corn & Onion Casserole

Tammy Wright
Decatur, TX

A "must-have" at Thanksgiving.

1/2 c. butter
2 sweet onions, thickly sliced
   and separated into rings
8-oz. container sour cream
1 c. shredded Cheddar cheese,
   divided

7-oz. pkg. corn muffin mix
1 egg, beaten
1/2 c. milk
4 drops hot pepper sauce
14-3/4 oz. can creamed corn

Melt butter in a skillet; add onions and sauté until golden.
Remove from heat; stir in sour cream and 1/2 cup cheese.
Set aside. Combine muffin mix, egg, milk, sauce and corn in a
medium bowl; mix well. Turn muffin mixture into a greased
9"x9" baking pan. Top with onion mixture; sprinkle with
remaining cheese. Bake, uncovered, at 350 degrees for one
hour. Serves 6.

Give a familiar cheesy casserole extra zing...
simply try a different flavor of cheese like
Pepper Jack or sharp Cheddar.

Green Beans Supreme

Jackie Balla
Walbridge, OH

A different twist on an old favorite.

2 14-1/2 oz. cans green
    beans, drained
14-oz. can cream of
    mushroom soup
2 T. milk

1-1/2 T. ranch salad
    dressing mix
8-oz. pkg. sliced mushrooms
1 c. shredded Cheddar cheese
1/2 c. chopped cashews

Place beans in a greased one-quart casserole dish; set aside.
In a small bowl, mix together soup, milk and dressing mix.
Pour soup mixture over beans; set aside. In a small skillet
sprayed with non-stick vegetable spray, cook mushrooms until
golden and lightly crunchy. Spoon mushrooms over soup mixture;
top with cheese and cashews. Bake, uncovered, at 350 degrees
for 20 minutes, until heated through. Makes 4 servings.

A container of sour cream will stay fresh & tasty
longer if you stir in a teaspoon or two of
white vinegar after first opening it.

Candied Sweet Potatoes

Chris Revennaugh
Mentor, OH

We love this clever way to fix an old stand-by,
using an oven roasting bag. There's no messy,
sticky clean-up...just toss away the bag!

1/4 c. all-purpose flour
4 sweet potatoes, peeled and
   thinly sliced
1/3 c. brown sugar, packed

1/4 c. margarine, sliced
2 T. maple-flavored pancake
   syrup
1/4 t. nutmeg

Shake flour in a large oven roasting bag; arrange bag in a
13"x9" baking pan. Toss sweet potatoes with remaining
ingredients to blend; arrange in an even layer in bag. Close
bag with nylon tie provided; cut six, 1/2-inch slits in top.
Tuck ends of bag into pan. Bake at 350 degrees for 45 minutes.
Serves 6 to 8.

Fragrant baking spices bring out the flavor in
sweet potatoes. Besides nutmeg, try adding a
little cinnamon, cloves, coriander or ginger...yummy!

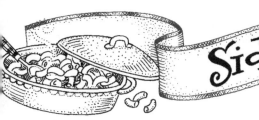
Nannie Raue's Sweet Potato Pone

Mary Rabon
Mobile, AL

My grandmother, Mary Raue, was the best cook ever! She always stayed up all night cooking for Christmas. I can remember her coming to our house and making this yummy side dish...it is a sweet memory for me.

6 c. sweet potatoes, peeled and grated
1/2 c. all-purpose flour
1 t. cinnamon
1 t. nutmeg
1-1/3 c. sugar

1 to 1-1/4 c. evaporated milk, divided
1 egg, beaten
6 T. butter, melted
1 t. vanilla extract

Combine sweet potatoes, flour, cinnamon, nutmeg and sugar in a large bowl. Add one cup evaporated milk; mix well. Stir in egg, blending well. Add butter and vanilla. Pour into a greased 13"x9" baking pan. Bake, uncovered, at 350 degrees for one hour and 30 minutes, stirring frequently. Add more milk if dry. Cut into squares; serve hot or cold. Serves 8 to 10.

Sprinkle crumbled gingersnap cookies over sweet potato casseroles for a sweet, crunchy topping.

Scalloped Pineapple

Dollie Isaacson
Danville, IL

A friend shared this recipe when we were invited to her house for a hot dog roast. Now it's a favorite for family gatherings.

3 eggs
2 c. sugar
1 c. butter, melted
3/4 c. milk

20-oz. can pineapple chunks, drained
8 slices white bread, torn

Beat together eggs and sugar; stir in remaining ingredients in order given. Pour into a greased 11"x7" baking pan. Bake, uncovered, for 40 minutes at 350 degrees. Serves 6 to 8.

Cranberry-Pineapple Sauce

Nancy Hobbs
Pennington Gap, VA

Delicious with roast turkey or chicken.

2 15-oz. cans pineapple
     tidbits, drained and
     3/4 c. juice reserved
2 T. cornstarch
1 T. orange zest

1/4 t. ground cloves
1/4 t. nutmeg
16-oz. can whole-berry
     cranberry sauce

In a medium saucepan over medium heat, gradually stir reserved pineapple juice into cornstarch; mix until smooth. Add remaining ingredients except pineapple tidbits. Bring to a boil, stirring constantly. Lower heat and cook until thickened and translucent. Stir in pineapple. Serve warm or chilled. Makes 8 to 10 servings.

Pineapple Gelatin Salad

Mildred Selby
Russell Springs, KY

This recipe is special to me...it brings back memories of a dear friend.

8-oz. pkg. cream cheese,
  softened
6-oz. pkg. lemon-lime gelatin
  mix
2 c. boiling water

20-oz. can crushed pineapple
1/2 to 1 c. chopped walnuts
1 t. vanilla extract
1 t. sugar
3/4 to 1 c. lemon-lime soda

Beat cream cheese until creamy; set aside. Stir gelatin mix into boiling water until dissolved; gradually add to cream cheese. Add remaining ingredients except soda; mix well. Slowly add soda. Pour into a glass serving dish. Chill until set, about 2 hours. Serves 8 to 10.

Let gelatin set to semi-firm, about the consistency of cold egg whites, before adding fruit pieces and mini marshmallows. Then push them right in... they won't float or sink!

Mom's Zucchini Casserole

Karen Puchnick
Lyndora, PA

My dear mother has made this wonderful recipe for years. She used to deep-fry the zucchini, but now she makes this healthier version. I'm not fond of zucchini, but I love this stuff!

2 eggs
1 c. seasoned dry bread
   crumbs
1/2 t. garlic powder
1/4 t. celery salt
2 T. grated Parmesan cheese

2 to 3 zucchini, sliced
2 to 3 tomatoes, sliced
garlic powder and dried
   oregano to taste
1/2 lb. sliced mozzarella
   cheese

Lightly beat eggs in a shallow dish; set aside. In a second dish, mix bread crumbs with garlic powder, celery salt and Parmesan cheese. Dip zucchini slices into egg, then into crumb mixture. Arrange zucchini on a greased baking sheet. Bake at 350 degrees for 10 to 15 minutes, until golden; turn over and bake an additional 10 to 15 minutes. Layer half of zucchini in a greased 13"x9" baking pan; top with half of tomatoes, garlic powder and oregano to taste and half the mozzarella. Repeat layers, ending with mozzarella. Bake, uncovered, at 350 degrees for 15 to 20 minutes, or until heated through. Serves 6 to 8.

Use Mom's vintage baking dishes from the 1950's to serve up casseroles with sweet memories. If you don't have any of hers, keep an eye open at tag sales and thrift stores...you may find the very same kind of dishes she used!

Baked Spinach & Rice

Elena Smith
Seaside, CA

*I find this casserole is just as tasty if I substitute 4 egg whites
for the whole eggs and use a "light" cheese spread.*

10-oz. pkg. frozen spinach,
    cooked and well drained
2 c. cooked rice
8-oz. pkg. pasteurized process
    cheese spread, cubed
1/3 c. onion, chopped

1/3 c. red pepper, chopped
3 eggs, beaten
1/8 t. pepper
Optional: 1/4 lb. turkey bacon,
    crisply cooked and
    crumbled

Combine all ingredients; mix well. Spread in a greased
10"x6" baking pan; smooth top with a spatula. Bake, uncovered,
at 350 degrees for 30 minutes. Let stand for 5 minutes; cut into
squares. Makes 8 to 10 servings.

To keep rice from becoming sticky, don't stir it
after cooking. Instead, gently fluff it with a fork.
It works every time!

7-Layer Salad

Beverly Mock
Pensacola, FL

*A potluck-perfect salad...I like to tell everyone its name
and see if they can identify all seven layers.*

1 head lettuce, torn
1 head cauliflower, coarsely
   chopped
10-oz. pkg. frozen peas,
   thawed
1 bunch green onions,
   chopped

1/2 lb. bacon, crisply cooked
   and crumbled
.7-oz. pkg. Italian salad
   dressing mix
2 c. mayonnaise

In a large bowl, layer ingredients except mayonnaise in the order
given. Spoon mayonnaise over top and seal to edges. Cover and
refrigerate overnight. Serve layered or toss before serving.
Serves 8 to 10.

Enjoy all the scrumptious flavor of bacon with none
of the mess! Lay bacon slices on a jelly-roll pan
and bake at 350 degrees for 15 to 20 minutes, until
it's as crisp as you like. Drain well on paper towels.

Warm German Potato Salad

Debra Manley
Bowling Green, OH

A fall favorite at our house...delicious with grilled bratwurst.

3/4 lb. bacon, diced
2 T. onion, diced
2 T. vinegar
3/4 c. mayonnaise

8 redskin potatoes, cooked
  and thickly sliced
6 eggs, hard-boiled, peeled
  and chopped

In a large skillet over medium heat, cook bacon and onion until bacon is crisp. Drain, reserving 1/4 cup drippings. Add vinegar and mayonnaise to drippings; stir until blended. Stir in potatoes and eggs; toss lightly. Serve warm. Serves 6 to 8.

Kickin' Chili Fries

Coleen Lambert
Casco, WI

Hearty chili and melting cheese over French fries...yum!

32-oz. pkg. frozen French fries
15-oz. can chili without beans

8-oz. jar pasteurized process
  cheese sauce

Fry or bake French fries as package directs; place on a serving platter and keep warm. Heat chili and cheese sauce separately, as packages direct. Spoon hot chili over potatoes; top with hot cheese sauce and serve immediately. Makes 8 servings.

Sweet Onion Dip

Beth Kramer
Port Saint Lucie, FL

*The mild flavor of the onion really shines through
in this simple recipe.*

2 c. sweet onion, chopped   2 c. shredded Swiss cheese
2 c. mayonnaise

Mix together all ingredients; spread in a lightly greased 8"x8"
baking pan. Bake, uncovered, at 350 degrees for 20 minutes,
until golden and bubbly. Makes 6 cups.

Hot Chili Cheese Dip

David Wink
Gooseberry Patch

*A make-ahead favorite! I like to chill this dip overnight so
that the flavors can blend, then reheat it at serving time.*

1 lb. mild or spicy ground pork   14-1/2 oz. can tomatoes with
   sausage, browned and   chiles
   drained   16-oz. pkg. pasteurized
2 10-3/4 oz. cans nacho   process cheese spread,
   cheese soup   cubed
15-oz. can chili without beans

Combine all ingredients except cheese in a large saucepan over
medium heat; cook until bubbly. Add cheese. Reduce heat; cook
and stir until cheese is completely melted. Makes 6 to 7 cups.

Too much of a good thing
is wonderful.

-Mae West

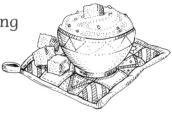

Homemade Guacamole

Athena Colegrove
Big Springs, TX

The buttery flavor of ripe avocados makes guacamole my
favorite comfort food...I could eat the whole bowl myself!

6 avocados, halved and pitted
2 to 4 cloves garlic, minced
1 lime, halved and divided
1 tomato, diced
1/2 onion, diced

salt to taste
Optional: 1 diced jalapeño
  pepper, chopped fresh
  cilantro

Scoop avocados into a large bowl. Add garlic and juice of 1/2 lime; mash to desired consistency. Gently stir in tomato, onion, salt and juice of remaining 1/2 lime; add jalapeño and cilantro, if using. Cover and chill for 30 minutes to one hour; stir again before serving. Makes 6 to 8 servings.

Try serving "light" dippers with hearty full-flavored dips and spreads. Fresh veggies, pita wedges, baked tortilla chips and multi-grain crispbread are all sturdy enough to scoop up dips yet won't overshadow the flavor of the dip.

Broccoli & Cheese Squares

Lori VanAntwerp
Gooseberry Patch

An old friend shared this recipe...she served this at all her family get-togethers. It is fast and easy, not to mention tasty!

3 T. butter
3 eggs
1 c. milk
1 c. all-purpose flour
1 t. salt
1 t. baking powder

2 12-oz. pkgs. shredded mild Cheddar cheese
2 10-oz. pkgs. frozen chopped broccoli, cooked and drained
2 t. onion, chopped

Melt butter in a 13"x9" baking pan; tilt to coat bottom and set aside. Beat eggs in a large mixing bowl. Add milk, flour, salt and baking powder; mix well. Stir in cheese, broccoli and onion; spoon into pan. Bake, uncovered, at 350 degrees until set, 30 to 35 minutes. Cut into squares. Serves 8 to 10.

Steamy hot baked potatoes...almost a meal in themselves! Scrub potatoes and pierce them with a fork. Rub with olive oil and roll lightly in coarse salt for yummy skins. Bake for 60 minutes at 350 degrees, placing potatoes on middle oven rack and turning over once. Scrumptious!

Mains

Mom's favorite pot roast recipe... the perfect Sunday dinner.

Cheesy Beef & Bacon Burger Meatloaf *Kelly Masten*
Hudson, NY

Growing up in a large family, we ate a lot of meatloaf.
This recipe always kept us coming back for more!

1 lb. bacon, crisply cooked,
    crumbled and divided
1-1/2 lbs. ground beef sirloin
1-1/2 c. shredded Cheddar
    cheese
2 eggs, beaten
1/3 c. bread crumbs

1/3 c. mayonnaise
1 T. Worcestershire sauce
1/2 t. salt
1/2 t. pepper
1/2 c. catsup
1/4 t. hot pepper sauce
3 T. Dijon mustard

Set aside 1/2 cup bacon for topping. Combine remaining bacon, ground beef, cheese, eggs, crumbs, mayonnaise, Worcestershire sauce, salt and pepper in a large bowl; set aside. Mix together catsup, hot sauce and mustard; set aside 3 tablespoons of mixture. Add remaining catsup mixture to beef mixture; blend well. Press into an ungreased 9"x5" loaf pan; spread reserved catsup mixture over top and sprinkle with reserved bacon. Bake, uncovered, at 350 degrees for 50 to 60 minutes, until done. Remove from oven; let stand 5 to 10 minutes before slicing. Serves 6 to 8.

The most indispensible ingredient of all good home
cooking...love, for those you are cooking for.

-Sophia Loren

Janet's Awesome Meatloaf

Michelle Namminga
Gainesville, VA

My mom knew I absolutely loved her meatloaf. Whenever I was sick or just feeling blue, she would make this for me and it always made me smile. Now I make it for my children and they love it too!

3 lbs. ground beef
1-1/2 c. bread crumbs
1-1/2 c. favorite pasta sauce
1 c. onion, diced
3 cloves garlic, minced

1 T. dry mustard
1/8 t. nutmeg
1/8 t. pepper
4 slices bacon

Mix together all ingredients except bacon. Form into 2 loaves and place in an ungreased 13"x9" baking pan. Arrange 2 slices bacon over each loaf. Bake, uncovered, at 375 degrees for 45 minutes. Makes 12 servings.

For a lower-fat meatloaf, simply pat the meat mixture into a loaf shape and place it on a rimmed baking sheet. Any excess fat will run off as the meatloaf bakes.

Slow-Cooker Chicken & Dumplings
Rhonda Reeder
Ellicott City, MD

*With a slow cooker, you can serve your family a homestyle
dinner even after a busy day away from home.*

1-1/2 lbs. boneless, skinless
    chicken breasts, cubed
2 potatoes, cubed
2 c. baby carrots
2 stalks celery, sliced
2 10-3/4 oz. cans cream of
    chicken soup

1 c. water
1 t. dried thyme
1/4 t. pepper
2 c. biscuit baking mix
2/3 c. milk

Place chicken, potatoes, carrots and celery in a slow cooker; set
aside. In a medium bowl, combine soup, water, thyme and pepper;
pour over chicken mixture. Cover and cook on low setting for 7 to
8 hours, until chicken is done. Mix together baking mix and milk;
drop into slow cooker by large spoonfuls. Tilt lid to vent and cook
on high setting for 30 minutes, until dumplings are cooked in
center. Serves 8.

Homemade herb dumplings...yum! Just
add a teaspoon of snipped fresh parsley,
rosemary or thyme to the biscuit mix.

Chilly-Day Chicken Pot Pie

Jessica McAlister
Fort Worth, TX

This is my family's favorite chicken pot pie recipe...
everyone who tries it asks me for the recipe.

2 9-inch pie crusts
1/4 c. margarine
1/4 c. all-purpose flour
1/4 t. poultry seasoning
1/8 t. pepper

1 c. chicken broth
2/3 c. milk
2 c. cooked chicken, cubed
2 c. frozen mixed vegetables,
    thawed

Place one crust in an ungreased 9" pie plate; set aside.
Melt margarine in a saucepan over medium heat; stir in flour,
seasoning and pepper. Cook until mixture is smooth and
bubbly. Gradually add broth and milk; bring to a boil. Reduce
heat and simmer, stirring constantly until mixture thickens. Stir
in chicken and vegetables; cook until heated through. Pour into
pie plate. Place second crust over filling; crimp edges and cut
vents in top. Bake at 400 degrees for 20 to 30 minutes, until
golden. Serves 4.

Cut vents in your pot pie crust with a
chicken-shaped mini cookie cutter...so sweet.

Sunday Beef & Noodles

Peggy Donnally
Toledo, OH

Noodles and potatoes...that's my idea of heaven on a plate!

2-lb. beef chuck roast
4 c. beef broth
1 c. onion, chopped
2 t. onion powder
1 t. garlic powder

1 T. dried parsley
salt and pepper to taste
16-oz. pkg. extra wide egg
   noodles, cooked
mashed potatoes

Place roast in a slow cooker. Combine broth, onion and seasonings; pour over roast. Cover and cook on low setting for 6 to 8 hours. Remove roast; slice and return to slow cooker. Add noodles to slow cooker; heat through. Serve over mashed potatoes. Serves 6 to 8.

Beef Tips with Rice

Wendy Sensing
Franklin, TN

This is one of my family's favorite old stand-bys.
It's great to fix when taking a meal to a friend too.

1-1/2 lbs. stew beef, cubed
10-3/4 oz. can cream of
   mushroom soup

10-1/2 oz. can French onion
   soup
cooked rice

Combine all ingredients except rice in a slow cooker. Cover and cook on low setting for 6 hours, or on high setting for 4 hours. Serve over cooked rice. Serves 6 to 8.

Pour a tablespoon or two of cider vinegar
over beef before roasting or stewing...even
the toughest meat will cook up fork-tender.

Mains

Salmon Patties

Beverly Dunn
New Palestine, IN

*My mother gave me this recipe when I was
a young wife...it's still always a hit.*

14-3/4 oz. can salmon,
   drained and 2 T. liquid
   reserved
1 egg, beaten
1/3 c. onion, minced

1/4 c. all-purpose flour
2 t. baking powder
oil for frying
salt and pepper to taste

Combine salmon, egg, onion and flour in a medium bowl; set
aside. In a small bowl, mix together reserved salmon liquid and
baking powder; stir into salmon mixture. Form into 4 patties.
Heat oil in a large skillet over medium heat; add patties. Cook
until golden on both sides. Sprinkle with salt and pepper.
Makes 4 servings.

Chinese Tuna Noodle Casserole

Beth Bennett
Stratham, NH

*My mother-in-law Dorothy was a wonderful cook. She came
up with this recipe when she had 5 kids to feed...it's delicious!*

2 10-3/4 oz. cans cream of
   mushroom soup
2 6-oz. cans tuna, drained

2 12-oz. cans chow mein
   noodles
2 to 3 c. milk

Combine soup, tuna and noodles, being careful not to crush
noodles. Pour into a greased 2-quart casserole dish. Add
enough milk to come to top of noodles. Bake, uncovered,
at 350 degrees for 35 to 45 minutes, until hot and bubbly
and top of casserole is crunchy and golden. Serves 4 to 6.

Pot Roast & Dumplings

Wendy Sensing
Franklin, TN

This is one of our favorite meals on a cold winter day. If you cook the roast overnight, you can make the dumplings the next morning. At the end of a busy day, dinner is practically ready!

2 c. baby carrots
5 potatoes, peeled and halved
4-lb. beef chuck roast

garlic salt and pepper to taste
2 c. water
1-oz. pkg. onion soup mix

Arrange carrots and potatoes in a slow cooker. Place roast on top; sprinkle with garlic salt and pepper. In a small bowl, stir together water and soup mix; pour over roast. Cover and cook on low setting for 6 to 8 hours. Drain most of broth from slow cooker into a large soup pot; keep roast and vegetables warm in slow cooker. Bring broth to a boil over medium-high heat. Drop dumpling batter into boiling broth by teaspoonfuls. Cover and cook for 15 minutes. Serve dumplings with sliced roast and vegetables. Makes 8 to 10 servings.

Dumplings:

2 c. all-purpose flour
1/2 t. salt

3 T. baking powder
1 c. light cream

Sift together dry ingredients. Add cream and stir quickly to make a medium-soft batter.

Let roasts stand for a few minutes before slicing, so all of the savory juices can reabsorb into the meat.

Pork & Sauerkraut Stew

Karen Pilcher
Burleson, TX

This stew conjures up warm and comforting memories of growing up in the Midwest. It has a really good flavor and the meat is so tender.

2 14-oz. cans sauerkraut,
   drained
3 lbs. country-style pork ribs
4 c. cabbage, shredded
2 c. onion, coarsely chopped
2 T. brown sugar, packed
2 T. Worcestershire sauce

1-1/2 oz. pkg. onion soup
   mix
1 t. caraway seed
1-1/2 c. water
1-1/2 lbs. redskin potatoes,
   peeled and sliced

Spread sauerkraut in a large Dutch oven; add pork, cabbage and onion. Set aside. In a medium bowl, stir together remaining ingredients except potatoes; add to Dutch oven. Bring to a boil over medium-high heat; reduce heat and simmer for 2-1/2 hours, stirring occasionally. Add potatoes; cover and continue to simmer until potatoes are tender, about one hour. Serves 6.

When cooking cabbage or sauerkraut, do as Mom did...lay a heel of bread on top before covering the pot, and there will be no cabbage odor! Afterwards, just toss out the bread.

Momma's Shepherd's Pie

Barb Scott
Bowling Green, IN

*This recipe is very quick to prepare, looks delicious and
tastes even better...my family loves it!*

1-1/2 lbs. ground beef,
   browned and drained
15-oz. can cream of
   mushroom soup
14-1/2 oz. can green beans,
   drained
15-1/4 oz. can corn, drained

4 servings mashed potatoes
2 eggs, beaten
1/2 c. grated Parmesan cheese
1-1/2 c. shredded sharp
   Cheddar cheese
1/2 c. Colby cheese, shredded

Mix together ground beef and soup; spread in an ungreased
9"x9" baking pan. Layer beans over top; spread corn over
beans. Combine potatoes, eggs and Parmesan cheese; spread
over vegetables. Top with shredded cheeses. Bake, covered, at
375 degrees for 45 minutes. Let stand for 10 minutes before
serving. Serves 4.

What a time-saver! Most casseroles can be prepared
the night before...just cover and refrigerate. Simply
add 15 to 20 minutes to the original baking time.

Stuffed Green Peppers & Meatballs *Denise Allison*
Gig Harbor, WA

This recipe was passed down from my grandmother Dora to my mother Pat and now to me. We grew up eating these on cold Midwest evenings over mashed potatoes. They always warmed us up!

10-3/4 oz. can tomato soup
1-1/4 c. water
1 c. instant rice, uncooked
1 lb. ground beef
1 egg, beaten
2 t. onion, grated

2 t. salt
pepper to taste
1/3 c. Italian bread crumbs
6 green peppers, tops
   removed and reserved

Stir together soup and water; set aside. Combine remaining ingredients except peppers in a large bowl; add 1/3 cup soup mixture and mix well. Stuff peppers with about 2/3 cup meat mixture; replace tops on peppers. Shape remaining meat mixture into 2-inch meatballs. Arrange peppers in a lightly greased large soup pot; add meatballs around peppers. Spoon remaining soup mixture over peppers and meatballs. Bring to a boil over medium heat. Reduce heat and simmer, covered, for 35 to 45 minutes, basting occasionally with soup mixture in pot. Makes 6 servings.

Herb-flavored stuffing mix makes a tasty topping for casseroles. Just place it in a plastic zipping bag and crush it quickly with a rolling pin...clever!

Chicken Cashew Casserole

Doris Wilson
Denver, IA

This is so easy, fast to make and best of all...yummy!

2 10-3/4 oz. cans cream of
    mushroom soup
2/3 c. water
2 c. cooked chicken, diced
1 c. celery
1/2 c. onion, grated
6-oz. container cashews

6-oz. can sliced water
    chestnuts, drained and
    coarsely chopped
4-oz. can sliced mushrooms,
    drained
2 5-oz. cans chow mein
    noodles

Combine all ingredients except one can noodles. Spread in a lightly greased 13"x9" baking pan. Bake, uncovered, at 350 degrees for 30 minutes. Sprinkle with remaining noodles; bake for an additional 10 minutes. Serves 6.

For a crispy, crunchy casserole topping, leave
the casserole dish uncovered while it's baking.
Cover it only if you prefer a softer consistency.

Johnny Marzetti

Laura Fuller
Fort Wayne, IN

*Yum...this takes me right back to
grade-school lunch in the cafeteria.*

1 lb. ground beef
1 onion, chopped
4-oz. can sliced mushrooms,
   drained
1/8 t. garlic salt
pepper to taste
1-1/2 T. sugar

2 15-oz. cans tomato sauce
1 T. Worcestershire sauce
8-oz. pkg. wide egg noodles,
   cooked and divided
8-oz. pkg. shredded sharp
   Cheddar cheese

Cook ground beef, onion and mushrooms in a large skillet
over medium heat; drain. Stir in garlic salt, pepper, sugar
and sauces; simmer over low heat for 30 minutes. Layer half
the noodles in a greased 2-quart casserole dish. Follow with a
layer each of sauce and shredded cheese. Repeat layers. Bake,
uncovered, at 375 degrees for 20 to 30 minutes. Serves 4.

So many favorite comfort-food recipes begin with
pasta or noodles. The secret to perfectly cooked
pasta is to use plenty of cooking water...about
a gallon per pound of pasta, in a very large pot.

Mamaw's Cheesy Chicken Casserole   *Karen Sowers*
Lerna, IL

*My mamaw made this frequently and taught me to
make it when I was first married. It has become one
of my family's favorite meals.*

8-oz. pkg. elbow macaroni,
  cooked
2 10-3/4 oz. cans cream of
  chicken soup
1-1/2 c. whipping cream
2 boneless, skinless chicken
  breasts, cooked and cubed

4 eggs, hard-boiled, peeled
  and diced
8-oz. pkg. shredded sharp
  Cheddar cheese
salt and pepper to taste
1/2 to 3/4 c. corn flake cereal,
  crushed

Mix together all ingredients except cereal; spoon into a lightly
greased 4-quart casserole dish. Sprinkle cereal over top. Bake,
uncovered, at 350 degrees for one hour. Serves 6.

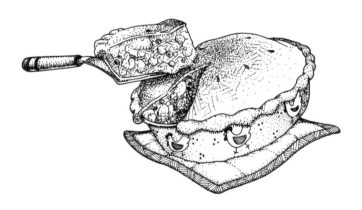

Chicken with twice the flavor! Let it cool in its
broth before cutting or shredding for casseroles.

Mom's Beef Stroganoff

*Wendy Lee Paffenroth
Pine Island, NY*

This is a good make-ahead dish...once the meat is tender, refrigerate it in its sauce. Reheat it at serving time and stir in the sour cream.

1/2 c. all-purpose flour
1 t. paprika
1 t. dry mustard
1 t. salt
1/2 t. pepper
1-1/2 lbs. stew beef, sliced
    into strips
1/4 c. olive oil
1 onion, thinly sliced
3/4 lb. sliced mushrooms

1 c. water
14-1/2 oz. can beef broth
1/2 t. browning and
    seasoning sauce
1/2 c. sour cream
8-oz. pkg. wide egg noodles,
    cooked
Garnish: paprika, dried
    parsley

Combine flour and seasonings in a large plastic zipping bag. Add beef; seal and shake until all the meat is coated. Remove meat; reserve flour in plastic zipping bag. Heat oil in a Dutch oven over medium heat; brown meat on all sides. Add onion and mushrooms; sauté. Sprinkle with reserved flour; stir to mix. Add water, broth and seasoning sauce; stir. Reduce heat; cook for about one hour, until sauce is thickened and meat is tender. Remove from heat; stir in sour cream. Place noodles in large serving dish; spoon meat mixture over noodles. Sprinkle with paprika and parsley. Serves 3 to 4.

Cut beef, chicken or pork into thin strips
or slices in a snap! Just freeze the meat
for 20 to 30 minutes before slicing.

Penne with Bacon & Garlic

Irene Robinson
Cincinnati, OH

This is so simple to fix...and the flavor is out of this world!

3/4 lb. bacon, crisply cooked, crumbled and 2 T. drippings reserved
1/2 c. sliced mushrooms
2 cloves garlic, minced
16-oz. pkg. penne pasta, cooked

1 c. grated Parmesan cheese
1 pt. whipping cream
1/2 t. pepper
1/2 c. green onion, sliced

Heat reserved drippings in a large skillet over medium heat. Add mushrooms and garlic; cook for 3 minutes, or until tender. Stir in pasta, cheese, cream and pepper; simmer over medium-low heat until sauce is thickened, stirring often. Stir in crumbled bacon and green onion; serve immediately. Serves 4 to 6.

Toss cooked pasta with a little olive oil, then set aside and keep warm. When it's time to add it to a favorite casserole recipe, you'll find the oil has kept the pasta from sticking together.

Mains

WWII Mess Hall Chili

Phyllis Peters
Three Rivers, MI

In 1947 I married an Army veteran and we attended Army reunions for many years. The group of men and wives are like family. One friend, a former mess sergeant, shared his best-ever recipe for chili...scaled down for home use. I hope you enjoy it!

1 lb. dried pinto beans	5 c. tomatoes, diced
2 lbs. onions, chopped	1/2 c. fresh parsley, snipped
1 lb. green peppers, chopped	1/2 c. chili powder
1/2 c. margarine, divided	2 t. cayenne pepper
1-1/2 T. oil, divided	1 T. salt
2 lbs. ground beef	1 t. cumin seed
1 lb. lean ground pork	

Place beans in a Dutch oven; cover with water and soak overnight. The next morning, drain water; cover beans with fresh water and cook over medium-low heat until nearly tender. In a skillet over medium heat, sauté onions and green peppers in half of the margarine and oil. Add remaining margarine and oil; sauté beef and pork until browned. Drain; add meat mixture and remaining ingredients to beans in Dutch oven. Simmer for one to 1-1/2 hours, until beans are tender. Skim off any fat before serving. Makes about 4 quarts.

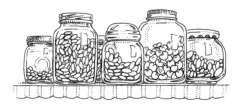

Don't worry if you forgot to soak the dried beans overnight! Use the quick-soak method...cover beans with water in a large saucepan and bring to a boil for 2 minutes. Remove from heat, cover and let the beans stand for 2 to 4 hours. Ready!

Grandma Shady's Ham Loaf

Debra Shady
Bluffton, IN

*We could always count on having ham loaf for dinner
when we went to Grandma's house. I believe the sauce
is what makes it oh-so good!*

2 lbs. baked ham
1-1/2 lbs. smoked ham
1-1/2 c. cracker crumbs

3 eggs, beaten
1-3/4 to 2 c. milk

Grind together baked and smoked ham in a food grinder. Add
crumbs, eggs and milk; mix well and shape into a loaf. Place in a
lightly greased 9"x5" loaf pan. Bake, uncovered, at 450 degrees for
20 minutes. Remove from oven and top with sauce; cover and
bake at 325 degrees for an additional 2 hours. Uncover shortly
before baking time is done; allow to brown slightly. Serves 8 to 10.

Sauce:

1 c. brown sugar, packed
3/4 c. vinegar

3/4 c. water
1 t. dry mustard

Combine ingredients and mix well.

Cut leftover meatloaf
into thick slices, wrap
individually and
freeze. Later, they
can be thawed and
rewarmed quickly
for scrumptious
meatloaf sandwiches
at a few moments' notice.

Lazy Pierogie

Kelly Alderson
Erie, PA

Hearty food for a cold winter's day.

15 lasagna noodles, cooked
   and divided
2 c. mashed potatoes
2 eggs, beaten
8-oz. pkg. shredded Cheddar
   cheese
garlic salt, pepper and onion
   powder to taste
1/2 c. butter
1 onion, chopped
Garnish: sour cream

Arrange 5 lasagna noodles in a lightly greased 13"x9 baking
pan; set aside. Combine potatoes, eggs, cheese and seasonings;
spread half of mixture over lasagna. Cover with another
5 lasagna noodles; spread with remaining potato mixture. Top
with remaining lasagna; set aside. Melt butter in a skillet over
medium heat; sauté onion until tender. Pour onion mixture
over lasagna. Cover with aluminum foil; bake at 350 degrees
for 30 minutes. Let stand for 10 minutes before slicing into
squares. Serve with sour cream on the side. Serves 4 to 6.

Did you know...onions can cause tomatoes and
potatoes to soften. Store onions away from other
produce, in a dark well-ventilated pantry.

Cheesy Ham Potatoes

Tricia Roberson
Waldorf, MD

This recipe cheers me right up! It tastes and smells like home at Grandma's...I think back to a wintry day in Kansas and see myself rubbing a spot in the frosted window to look outside.

32-oz. pkg. frozen diced
    potatoes
10-3/4 oz. can cream of
    potato soup
10-3/4 oz. can cream of
    celery soup
1 to 2 c. cooked ham, cubed
8-oz. container sour cream

2 green onions, chopped
1 c. milk
salt and pepper to taste
10-oz. pkg. sharp Cheddar
    cheese, shredded and
    divided

Combine all ingredients except cheese until well blended. Add half the cheese; stir well and spoon into a lightly greased 13"x9" baking pan. Bake, uncovered, at 350 degrees for one hour. Sprinkle with remaining cheese and bake for an additional 30 minutes. Let stand for 5 minutes before serving. Makes 8 servings.

A handy all-purpose seasoning to keep by the stove... simply mix 6 tablespoons salt and one tablespoon pepper and fill a large shaker. It's just right for sprinkling on pork chops, burgers, chicken and homestyle potatoes!

Mom's Meatballs

Keri Farris
Watseka, IL

This recipe came from my mom, who loved to cook more than anything. Everyone is eager to attend potlucks and parties when they hear we're bringing the meatballs!

6 to 8 slices bread
1 to 1-1/2 c. water
2 lbs. ground beef
1 lb. ground pork or turkey sausage
2 to 3 eggs, beaten
1 onion, chopped
1-1/2 t. garlic powder
1-1/2 t. dried oregano
1 t. salt
1 t. pepper
2 10-3/4 oz. cans cream of mushroom soup
8-oz. container sour cream
1 c. milk
1-1/2 oz. pkg. onion soup mix

Soak bread in water; tear into pieces. Combine meat, eggs, bread, onion and seasonings; form into 2-inch balls. Brown meatballs in a large skillet over medium heat, turning to cook evenly on all sides. Drain; transfer to a slow cooker and set aside. Combine remaining ingredients in a saucepan over low heat; stir until smooth. Cook until heated through and pour over meatballs. Cover and cook on low setting for 2 to 3 hours, stirring every 30 minutes. Serves 10 to 12.

Watch for old cast iron skillets at barn sales...they're worth their weight in gold. Often they just need a light scrub, then re-season by brushing lightly with oil and baking at 350 degrees for one hour. Let cool in the oven...all ready to use!

Newlywed Pork Chops

Stella Hickman
Gooseberry Patch

*I first tried this tasty, never-fail recipe years ago
when I was newly married. I hope you'll enjoy it too!*

4 boneless pork chops
1/2 t. garlic salt
1/8 t. pepper
1 onion, sliced

1 lemon, thinly sliced
4 t. dark brown sugar, packed
1/2 c. catsup

Arrange pork chops in a single layer in a lightly greased
1-1/2 quart casserole dish; sprinkle with garlic salt and pepper.
Top each pork chop with a slice each of onion and lemon; sprinkle
with one teaspoon brown sugar. Drizzle catsup over pork chops.
Cover and bake at 375 degrees for 45 minutes. Uncover; bake for
15 additional minutes. Makes 4 servings.

Always use tongs to turn chops and chicken pieces
in the pan. A fork pierces the meat, causing the
savory juices to run out.

Chicken & Wild Rice Casserole

Karen Lehmann
New Braunfels, TX

The ultimate comfort food casserole! Try it with leftover turkey too, when you have Thanksgiving leftovers and house guests to feed.

1/4 c. butter
1 onion, chopped
4 stalks celery, chopped
8-oz. can sliced water
  chestnuts, drained
2 6.2-oz. pkgs. long-grain &
  wild rice mix, prepared
5 c. cooked chicken, chopped

16-oz. pkg. shredded
  Cheddar cheese, divided
2 10-3/4 oz. cans cream of
  mushroom soup
16-oz. container sour cream
1 c. milk
1/2 t. salt
1/2 c. bread crumbs

Melt butter in a large skillet over medium heat. Add onion, celery and water chestnuts; sauté 10 minutes, or until tender. Stir in rice, chicken, 3 cups cheese, soup, sour cream, milk and salt. Spoon in a lightly greased 13"x9" baking pan; sprinkle with bread crumbs. Bake, uncovered at 350 degrees for 30 minutes. Sprinkle with remaining cheese and bake for an additional 5 minutes. Serves 8.

As soon as a casserole dish is empty, pop it into a sink full of hot, soapy water to speed clean-up...saves oodles of scrubbing time!

Susan's Slow-Cookin' Ribs

Susan Ice
Snohomish, WA

These ribs are so easy and versatile that I always make a double batch and freeze one. They can be eaten as is, or shredded and used for sandwiches. They melt in your mouth!

1 T. onion powder
1 t. red pepper flakes
1/2 t. dry mustard
1/2 t. garlic powder
1/2 t. allspice
1/2 t. cinnamon

3 lbs. boneless pork ribs, sliced into serving-size pieces
1 onion, sliced and divided
1/2 c. water
2 c. hickory-flavored barbecue sauce

Combine seasonings in a cup; mix well and rub over ribs. Arrange one-third of ribs in a layer in a slow cooker. Place one-third of onion slices over top; repeat layering. Pour water over top. Cover and cook on low setting for 8 to 10 hours. Drain and discard liquid from slow cooker. Pour barbecue sauce over ribs. Cover and cook on low setting for an additional one to 2 hours. Serves 6 to 8.

Boo hoo...don't let an onion make you cry!
Place it in the freezer for just 5 minutes
before chopping...no more tears.

Desserts

All desserts are wonderful...
à la mode!

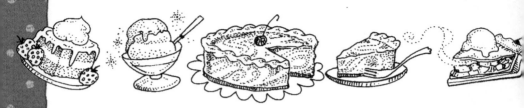

Chocolate Gooey Cake

Jennie Gist
Gooseberry Patch

*A creamy, caramel, chocolatey cake that's perfect
for sharing at potlucks and family dinners.*

18-1/4 oz. pkg. German
  chocolate cake mix
14-oz. can sweetened
  condensed milk
12-oz. jar caramel ice cream
  topping

8-oz. container frozen
  whipped topping, thawed
3 1.4-oz. chocolate toffee
  candy bars, crushed

Prepare cake according to package directions; bake in a greased
13"x9" baking pan. While cake is still warm, poke holes about
1/2 inch apart with a wooden spoon handle. Pour condensed milk
over cake; let stand for a few minutes and drizzle with caramel
topping. Spread with whipped topping; sprinkle with crushed
candy. Refrigerate 2 hours to overnight before serving; keep
refrigerated. Makes 16 servings.

Here's a slick trick for cutting a cake with sticky
frosting! Between slices, simply dip the knife in
hot water and wipe it clean with a paper towel.

Chocolate-Peanut Butter Squares

Diana Spray
Medora, IN

A no-bake treat that's almost child's play to make.

1-1/2 c. butter, divided
18-oz. jar crunchy peanut butter
1-1/2 c. graham cracker crumbs

2 c. powdered sugar
12-oz. pkg. chocolate chips

Melt one cup butter in microwave; stir in peanut butter until smooth. Add graham cracker crumbs and powdered sugar; stir until well blended. Press into a lightly greased 15"x10" jelly-roll pan; set aside. Combine chocolate chips and remaining butter in a microwave-safe bowl; microwave on high setting until melted. Stir until smooth and spread over peanut butter mixture. Chill until firm; cut into squares. Makes about 12 to 15.

Spray the measuring cup with non-stick vegetable spray before measuring honey or peanut butter... the sticky stuff will slip right out.

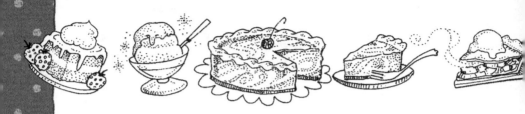

Old-Fashioned Bread Pudding

Charlene McCain
Bakersfield, CA

When the weather is cold outside, nothing brings the family in faster than the aroma of bread pudding baking in the oven.

10 slices white bread, cubed
1/4 c. butter, melted
1/2 c. raisins
1 t. cinnamon
3/4 c. sugar
6 eggs, beaten

2 t. vanilla extract
1/2 t. salt
3 c. milk
1/8 t. nutmeg
Garnish: whipped topping

Combine bread cubes, butter, raisins and cinnamon. Mix well; spread in a lightly greased 2-quart casserole dish. In a medium bowl, blend together sugar, eggs, vanilla and salt until sugar is dissolved. Add milk; beat well. Pour over bread mixture; let stand for 5 minutes. Sprinkle with nutmeg. Bake, uncovered, at 375 degrees for 25 minutes. Cool slightly before serving. Garnish with dollops of whipped topping. Serves 8.

Fresh whipped cream is oh-so easy to make. Combine one cup heavy cream with 1/4 cup powdered sugar and one teaspoon vanilla extract in a chilled bowl. Beat with chilled beaters until stiff peaks form. Dollop on a big slice of cake or pie...yummy!

Creamy Banana Pudding

Liz Gatewood
Madison, IN

My dear friend Barb gave me this recipe many years ago...
I think of her every time I make it.

5-1/4 oz. pkg. instant vanilla
   pudding mix
2 c. milk
14-oz. can sweetened
   condensed milk

12-oz. container frozen
   whipped topping, thawed
12-oz. pkg. vanilla wafers
4 to 5 bananas, sliced

Combine pudding mix, milks and topping in a large bowl; mix together until well blended. Spoon one cup of pudding mixture into a large glass serving bowl. Layer with one-third each of wafers, banana slices and remaining pudding mixture. Repeat layers twice, ending with pudding mixture. Chill; keep refrigerated. Makes 8 to 10 servings.

Make a good thing even better...sprinkle toasted coconut over Creamy Banana Pudding. Spread shredded coconut in a shallow pan and bake at 350 degrees for 7 to 12 minutes, stirring frequently, until toasted and golden.

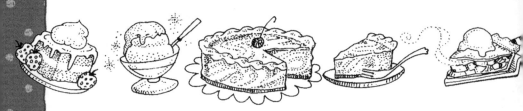

Chewy Chocolate Chip Cookies
Kathy Zimmerman
Burley, WA

Everyone's favorite! Whenever I take these to family gatherings, everyone raves about them. The secret...use shortening rather than butter or margarine and don't bake them too long.

3/4 c. shortening
1 c. sugar
1 c. brown sugar, packed
2 eggs
1 t. vanilla extract
2-1/2 c. all-purpose flour

1 t. baking soda
1 t. salt
12-oz. pkg. semi-sweet
    chocolate chips
1/2 c. chopped nuts

Blend together shortening, sugars, eggs and vanilla. Add flour, baking soda and salt; mix well. Stir in chocolate chips and nuts. Drop by rounded tablespoonfuls onto ungreased baking sheets. Bake at 375 degrees for 10 to 12 minutes (do not overbake). Cool on a wire rack. Makes 4 to 5 dozen.

Keep crisp cookies crisp and soft cookies chewy
in a cookie jar or tin...separate the layers
with sheets of wax paper.

Chocolate Chip Cheesecake Squares

Cindy Windle
White Hall, AR

Everyone loves this easy-to-make cheesecake.
When I take it to potlucks at church and office
events, there are never any leftovers!

2 18-oz. tubes refrigerated
    chocolate chip cookie dough,
    sliced 1/4-inch thick
    and divided

2 c. sugar
3 eggs, beaten
2 8-oz. pkgs. cream cheese,
    softened

Arrange half the cookie dough slices in a greased 13"x9" baking pan; press together to form crust and set aside. Combine sugar, eggs and cream cheese; beat until smooth. Spread over sliced cookies. Arrange remaining cookie dough slices over cream cheese mixture. Bake at 350 degrees for 45 minutes to one hour, until golden. Cut into squares. Serves 15.

When whisking ingredients in a bowl, a damp kitchen
towel can keep the mixing bowl in place. Just twist
the towel securely around the base of the bowl.

Grandma Bevy's Hot Fudge Sauce

Beverly Ray
Brandon, FL

I made this often when my children were young. We'd enjoy it drizzled over homemade cream puffs or vanilla ice cream. Now my daughter makes this ooey-gooey sauce for her little ones.

1 c. sugar	2 T. light corn syrup
2 T. baking cocoa	1 T. butter, diced
1/2 c. half-and-half	1/2 t. vanilla extract

Combine sugar and cocoa in a saucepan; stir in half-and-half. Add corn syrup and butter; mix well. Bring to a boil over medium heat, stirring constantly. Reduce heat; simmer for 10 minutes without stirring. Remove from heat; stir in vanilla. Tastes best when served immediately, but may be refrigerated and reheated when ready to serve. Makes about 1-1/2 cups.

Easy Chocolate Frosting

Kathie Hardina
Spring Hill, FL

A fudgy delight!

1/2 c. milk	2 c. sugar
1/2 c. butter, sliced	1 c. semi-sweet chocolate chips

Combine milk, butter and sugar in a saucepan over medium heat. Bring to a boil; cook for 30 seconds. Stir in chocolate chips. Remove from heat and set pan in cold water; stir slowly, being sure not to get water in frosting. Use immediately. Makes about enough to frost a 13"x9" cake or a 2-layer, 9-inch cake.

Counting calories? Try using applesauce instead of oil in brownie recipes. Applesauce makes brownies extra moist and works just as well as oil.

Desserts

Grandma's Chocolate Popcorn

Jayne Kohler
Elkhart, IN

I always helped my grandma make this great snack when I stayed at her house...now my kids really love it too!

14 c. popped popcorn
3 c. crispy rice cereal
Optional: 2 c. dry-roasted
   peanuts

1-1/2 lbs. melting chocolate,
   chopped
3 T. creamy peanut butter

In a large bowl, mix popcorn, cereal and peanuts, if using; set aside. Combine chocolate and peanut butter in a microwave-safe bowl. Microwave on high for 2 to 3 minutes until melted, stirring after every minute. Pour over popcorn mixture, tossing to coat well. Spread onto a large greased non-stick baking sheet; cool completely. Break apart; store in an airtight container up to 5 days. Makes about 20 to 22 cups.

Pennsylvania Peanut Butter Fudge

Gloria Sawtelle
Enfield, CT

Over 45 years ago, my neighbor gave me this recipe that her mother always made. Since then, I have made it many times for bake sales, for gifts and for my family. It is very good and oh-so easy.

18-oz. jar crunchy peanut butter
7-oz. jar marshmallow creme

16-oz. pkg. powdered sugar
1/2 c. water

Mix together peanut butter and marshmallow creme; set aside. Combine powdered sugar and water in a saucepan over medium heat. Bring to a boil; cook for 5 minutes. Pour into peanut butter mixture; beat well. Pour into a greased 9"x9" baking pan. Cool slightly; cut into one-inch squares while still warm. Makes about 5 dozen.

Chocolate Cobbler

Christy Bonner
Berry, AL

This is a treasured family recipe that has been passed down for many years...a rich, scrumptious treat for chocolate lovers!

3/4 c. margarine, melted
1-1/2 c. self-rising flour
2-1/2 c. sugar, divided
1/2 c. plus 1 T. baking cocoa,
    divided

3/4 c. milk
1 t. vanilla extract
2-1/4 c. boiling water

Spread margarine in a 13"x9" glass baking pan; set aside. Combine flour, one cup sugar, 3 tablespoons cocoa, milk and vanilla; pour into pan. Mix together remaining sugar and cocoa; sprinkle over top. Pour boiling water over top; do not stir. Bake at 350 degrees for 40 to 45 minutes. Makes 12 to 14 servings.

Mom's Chocolate Malt Shoppe Pie

Nancy Brush
Robinson, IL

We're a family of chocoholics and also love chocolate malts, so my mom created this pie that combines our 2 favorite things.

1-oz. pkg. sugar-free white
    chocolate instant pudding
    mix
4 to 5 t. chocolate malt powder
1 c. milk

8-oz. container frozen
    whipped topping, thawed
1-1/2 c. malted milk balls,
    crushed and divided
9-inch chocolate cookie crust

Mix together pudding, malt powder and milk. Fold in 3/4 of the whipped topping and 1-1/4 cups crushed candy; spread in crust. Spread with remaining topping. Sprinkle with remaining candy; chill until set. Serves 8.

Hello Dolly Bars

Marilyn Morel
Keene, NH

*My sister began making these in the late 1970's. Every time
I need a little pick-me-up I make these. My sister is no longer
with us, but these wonderful treats hold some very special
memories for me which I've passed down to my children
and now my grandson.*

1/2 c. margarine
1 c. graham cracker crumbs
1 c. sweetened flaked coconut
6-oz. pkg. semi-sweet chocolate
   chips
6-oz. pkg. butterscotch chips
14-oz. can sweetened
   condensed milk
1 c. chopped pecans

Mix together margarine and graham cracker crumbs; press into a
lightly greased 9"x9" baking pan. Layer with coconut, chocolate
chips and butterscotch chips. Pour condensed milk over top;
sprinkle with pecans. Bake at 350 degrees for 25 to 30 minutes.
Let cool; cut into bars. Makes 12 to 16 bars.

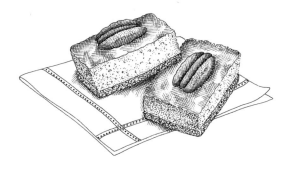

Be sure to use regular stick margarine in cookie recipes.
Reduced-fat margarine has a much higher water content
that will cause cookies not to bake up properly.

Baked Custard

Stephanie Mayer
Portsmouth, VA

*Creamy and comforting...top with a dollop of
whipped cream and a dash of nutmeg.*

1 c. evaporated milk
1 c. water
4 egg yolks

1/3 c. sugar
1/4 t. salt
1/2 t. vanilla extract

Combine milk and water in a saucepan; heat just to boiling
and set aside. Beat yolks slightly; add sugar, salt and vanilla.
Gradually add hot milk to eggs, stirring constantly. Divide into
4 custard cups; set in a pan of hot water. Bake at 325 degrees
for 50 minutes, or until a knife tip comes out clean. Serve warm
or chilled. Makes 4 servings.

Grandpa's Bread Pudding

Carolyn Helewski
Arcadia, FL

*Everyone loves this bread pudding! It's so simple to put together
and the fruit cocktail is a delicious, unexpected touch.*

2 eggs, beaten
1 c. sugar
2 c. milk
1 t. vanilla extract
10 slices bread, torn and
    divided

16-oz. can fruit cocktail,
    drained
2 T. butter, melted
Garnish: cinnamon

Mix together eggs, sugar, milk and vanilla; set aside. Arrange
half the bread in a greased 9"x5" loaf pan. Pour fruit over top;
cover with remaining bread. Pour egg mixture over top; drizzle
with butter and sprinkle with cinnamon. Bake at 350 degrees for
50 minutes. Serves 10 to 12.

Rice Pudding Just Like Grandma's

Jennifer Oglesby
Brownsville, IN

This recipe is so warm and comforting on a cold winter's day.

5 c. half-and-half
1 c. medium-grain long-cooking
   rice, uncooked
3/4 c. plus 2 T. sugar, divided
2 pasteurized egg yolks

1 t. vanilla extract
1-1/2 t. cinnamon, divided
2 T. butter, softened
3/4 c. golden raisins

Combine half-and-half and rice in a large saucepan over medium heat; bring to a boil. Reduce heat to low; simmer, stirring occasionally, for 10 minutes. Continue to simmer, stirring constantly, an additional 8 minutes, until rice is tender and creamy with some liquid left. Remove from heat; stir in 3/4 cup sugar, mixing well. In a small bowl, whisk together egg yolks, vanilla and 1/2 teaspoon cinnamon. Add 1/2 cup rice mixture, whisking to blend. Stir egg mixture into remaining rice mixture; mix well. Add butter and stir until evenly distributed. Pour into a serving bowl; cool to room temperature. Combine remaining sugar and cinnamon; sprinkle over pudding. Makes 4 servings.

You'll find uncooked eggs in many old-fashioned recipes, a practice that isn't recommended anymore. Look for eggs labeled as "pasteurized" to use in these recipes.

Black Bottom Cupcakes

Gretchen Brown
Forest Grove, OR

*Chocolate and cream cheese...what a scrumptious combination!
This recipe was given to me 15 years ago by a dear friend from
church as a wedding shower gift.*

2 8-oz. pkgs. cream cheese,
   softened
2 eggs, beaten
2-2/3 c. sugar, divided
1-1/4 t. salt, divided
1-1/2 c. semi-sweet chocolate
   chips

3 c. all-purpose flour
2 t. baking soda
1/2 c. baking cocoa
2 c. water
2/3 c. oil
2 T. vinegar
2 t. vanilla extract

Combine cream cheese, eggs, 2/3 cup sugar, 1/4 teaspoon salt
and chocolate chips; mix well and set aside. Combine remaining
ingredients in a large bowl. Fill paper-lined muffin tins 2/3 full; top
each with a heaping teaspoon of cream cheese mixture. Bake at
350 degrees for 25 to 30 minutes. Makes 2 dozen.

Stir up sweet memories...look through Grandma's
recipe box and rediscover a long-forgotten
favorite dessert recipe to share.

Desserts

Grandma's Banana Cupcakes

Kelly Marcum
Rock Falls, IL

My grandma used to make these often...they were so yummy!
I like to drizzle a little caramel sauce over the tops
to make them extra special.

1/2 c. butter
1-3/4 c. sugar
2 eggs
2 c. all-purpose flour
1 t. baking soda
1 t. baking powder

1 c. sour milk
2 bananas, mashed
1 t. vanilla extract
Optional: 1/2 c. chopped
   pecans

Blend butter for 5 minutes, using an electric mixer on medium speed. Slowly add sugar; beat in eggs. Add dry ingredients alternately with milk. Stir in bananas, vanilla and nuts, if using. Fill paper-lined muffin cups 1/2 full. Bake at 350 degrees for 18 to 25 minutes, until a toothpick inserted in the center comes out clean. Allow to cool; frost with Cream Cheese Frosting. Keep refrigerated after frosting. Makes 1-1/2 to 2 dozen.

Cream Cheese Frosting:

1/2 c. butter, softened
8-oz. pkg. cream cheese,
   softened

16-oz. pkg. powdered sugar
1 t. vanilla extract
1/8 t. salt

Blend all ingredients together until spreadable, using an electric mixer on medium speed.

If an old recipe calls for a cup of sour milk,
just stir a teaspoon of white vinegar into a cup
of fresh milk and let it stand for a few minutes.

Warm Apple Cake & Caramel Sauce *Stacie Mickley*
Gooseberry Patch

Warm out of the oven, drizzled with homemade
caramel sauce...very comforting!

1 c. all-purpose flour
1 c. sugar
1 t. baking soda
1 t. cinnamon
1/4 t. salt

1 egg, beaten
2 c. apples, cored, peeled and
    shredded
1/4 c. chopped walnuts

Combine flour, sugar, baking soda, cinnamon and salt in a large
bowl; set aside. Mix together egg and apples; add to flour mixture.
Stir in walnuts. Spread in a lightly greased 8"x8" baking pan. Bake
at 350 degrees for 25 to 30 minutes, until a toothpick inserted
near center comes out clean. Serve warm, drizzled with Caramel
Sauce. Makes 9 servings.

Caramel Sauce:

1/2 c. brown sugar, packed
2 T. all-purpose flour
1/8 t. salt

1 c. water
1 T. butter
1/4 t. vanilla extract

Combine brown sugar, flour and salt in a small saucepan.
Gradually add water; stir until smooth. Cook and stir over medium
heat until mixture comes to a boil. Cook for one to 2 minutes, until
thickened. Remove from heat; stir in butter and vanilla.

For delicious apple pies and
cakes, some of the best apple
varieties are Granny Smith,
Gala and Jonathan
as well as old-timers
like Rome Beauty,
Northern Spy & Winesap.

Comforting Southern Cake

Vivian Nikanow-Kaszuba
Chicago, IL

A slice of this scrumptious cake will make you feel much better!

18-1/2 oz. pkg. yellow cake mix
3.4-oz. pkg. vanilla-flavored
   instant pudding mix
4 eggs
1/2 c. cold water

1/2 c. oil
1/2 c. peach-flavored bourbon
   or orange juice
1-1/2 c. chopped nuts
Garnish: powdered sugar

Combine all ingredients except nuts and powdered sugar; beat for
3 minutes. Stir in nuts; pour batter into a greased and floured
Bundt® pan. Bake at 325 degrees for one hour. While cake is still
hot, poke holes all over with a toothpick; slowly pour glaze over
cake. Let cake cool in pan. Invert onto serving platter; sprinkle
with powdered sugar. Serves 10 to 12.

Glaze:

1/4 c. butter
2 T. water
1/2 c. sugar

1/4 c. peach-flavored bourbon
   or orange juice

Melt butter in a small saucepan over medium heat. Stir in water
and sugar; boil for 3 minutes, stirring constantly. Remove from
heat; stir in bourbon or orange juice.

Cut cake into cubes and layer in parfait glasses
with pudding, fruit or ice cream...a tasty
dessert just like Mom used to make.

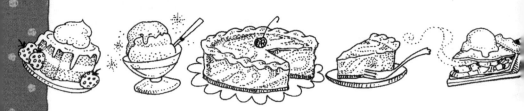

Great-Grandma's Pound Cake

Shelley Sullivan
Saint Clair, MO

My aunt won a blue ribbon at the Michigan State Fair with this cake recipe. It is so good, it doesn't even need frosting.

2 c. butter, softened
16-oz. pkg. powdered sugar
6 eggs

1 T. almond extract
3 c. all-purpose flour

Beat butter until light and fluffy; add powdered sugar, mixing well. Add eggs, one at a time, beating well after each addition. Add extract and flour; mix just enough to blend. Pour into a greased and floured 10" tube pan. Bake at 350 degrees for one hour and 15 minutes, or until cake tests done. Serves 8 to 10.

Debi's Homemade Vanilla Extract

Debi DeVore
Dover, OH

Oh-so easy...so much more flavorful than grocery store vanilla!

2 vanilla beans, split
lengthwise

1 c. vodka

Place vanilla beans in a jar with a lid; pour vodka over them. Seal; keep in a cool, dark place, shaking occasionally. Strain and rebottle after at least 3 to 5 weeks. Flavor is better if extract has steeped for 2 to 3 months before using. Makes one cup.

Stir up a sweet & easy topping to spoon over pound cake... just mix a pint of sliced ripe strawberries with 1/4 cup strawberry jam and 1/4 cup orange juice.

Chocolate Pound Cake

Sandy Groezinger
Stockton, IL

I've been using this recipe for years. It's super-moist...
all it needs is a dusting of powdered sugar.

12-oz. pkg. milk chocolate chips
1/2 c. butter, softened
2 c. sugar
4 eggs
2 t. vanilla extract
1 c. buttermilk

2 T. water
2-1/2 c. all-purpose flour
1/2 t. salt
1/4 t. baking soda
1/2 c. chopped walnuts
Garnish: powdered sugar

Melt chocolate in a saucepan over low heat; remove from heat and set aside. Beat together butter and sugar in a mixing bowl until light and fluffy. Add eggs, one at a time, beating well after each addition. Blend in melted chocolate and vanilla; set aside. Mix together buttermilk and water; set aside. Combine flour, salt and baking soda; add to chocolate mixture alternately with buttermilk mixture. Fold in nuts; pour into a greased and floured 10" tube pan. Bake at 325 degrees for 1-1/2 hours, or until a toothpick inserted near the center tests clean. Cool for 10 minutes; remove from pan to wire rack. Sprinkle with powdered sugar. Serves 12 to 16.

Brighten someone's day with a homemade cupcake tucked in their lunchbox! To pack the cupcake with no sticky mess, use a turkey baster to squirt the frosting down into the center of the cupcake.

Grandma Gregory's Buttermilk Pie *Becky Zepf-Piela*
Danbury, CT

*My grandmother's pie recipe is so old that it calls for
"a hunk of butter the size of an egg." I always make
this pie for Thanksgiving, just as she did.*

2 eggs
1-1/2 c. sugar
1/4 c. butter, softened
2-1/2 T. all-purpose flour

1 c. buttermilk
1 t. lemon extract
9-inch pie crust

Beat eggs, sugar, butter and flour together; stir in buttermilk
and extract. Pour into pie crust; bake at 400 degrees for 30 to
35 minutes, until set. Makes 6 to 8 servings.

Graham Cracker Pudding *Karen Rowell*
Berne, IN

*This was my mom's recipe and is so full of good memories!
It's comfort food to the max...it manages to taste both rich
and light and always takes me back to good times.*

20 graham cracker squares,
  crushed and divided
1 c. milk
1 c. sugar

.25-oz. env. unflavored gelatin
3 pasteurized eggs, separated
1 t. vanilla extract
1 c. whipping cream, whipped

Pat half the cracker crumbs into an ungreased 9"x9" baking pan;
set aside. Combine milk and sugar in a saucepan; sprinkle with
gelatin. Let stand for 30 minutes. Beat in egg yolks with an electric
mixer. Bring to a boil over medium heat; stir constantly until thickened. Chill; cool completely. Beat egg whites into soft peaks. Fold
egg whites and vanilla into whipped cream; fold into cooled gelatin
mixture. Gently spread over crumb mixture; sprinkle with
remaining crumbs. Chill at least 2 hours. Serves 8.

Comfort Foods
for
One or Two

...when just a bite will do!

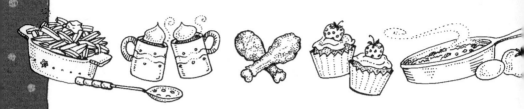

Sausage & Apple Skillet

Melanie Lowe
Dover, DE

*I like to serve this with crispy golden hashbrown patties
for a satisfying breakfast or supper.*

3 T. butter, divided
14-oz. pkg. fully cooked pork
   sausage, sliced
1 Granny Smith apple, cored,
   peeled and sliced

1 onion, sliced
1 c. apple cider
2 T. fresh sage, chopped
2 T. lemon juice
salt and pepper to taste

Melt one tablespoon butter in a skillet over medium heat; add
sausage. Cook until beginning to brown, about 5 minutes, turning
occasionally. Add apple and onion to skillet; sauté until tender and
golden, about 5 minutes, stirring often. Add cider and sage;
increase heat to high. Cook and stir for about 2 minutes; stir in
lemon juice, salt and pepper. With a slotted spoon, transfer apple
mixture to 2 plates; top with sausage. Whisk remaining butter into
skillet; drizzle over sausage. Makes 2 servings.

Enjoy your favorite comfort foods even if you have
a pint-size kitchen. With small appliances like
toaster ovens and mini slow cookers, you can
cook up just the right amount for one or two.

Corn & Bacon Chowder

Judy Voster
Neenah, WI

My husband's favorite! Sometimes I like to stir in some leftover diced chicken too.

2 slices bacon, diced
1/4 to 1/2 c. onion, chopped
14-oz. can chicken broth
1 c. potato, peeled and diced
1 c. creamed corn
salt and pepper to taste
Garnish: fresh parsley, chopped

Cook bacon over medium heat until almost crisp; add onion and cook until soft. Add broth, potato and corn; cover and bring to a boil. Reduce heat; simmer about 12 to 15 minutes, until potatoes are tender. Add salt and pepper to taste; garnish with parsley. Serves 2.

Treat yourself to one or two deviled eggs the no-mess way. Simply combine cooked egg yolks and fixin's in a small plastic zipping bag and squeeze to mix. Clip off a corner of the bag and squeeze the filling into egg whites, then toss away the bag.

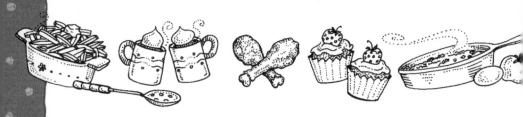

Dad's Famous BLT's

Tina Stidam
Delaware, OH

*My dad and I would pick the best tomato in the garden
for our BLT's...such delightful memories!*

4 slices bread or 2 English
   muffins, split and toasted
butter or mayonnaise to taste
2 leaves lettuce

1 tomato, sliced
salt and pepper to taste
4 slices Canadian-style bacon,
   crisply cooked

Spread bread or muffin halves on one side with butter or mayonnaise. Layer lettuce, tomato, salt, pepper and bacon on 2 pieces bread; top with remaining bread. Cut sandwiches in half. Serves 2.

Pita Tuna Melts

Melody Taynor
Everett, WA

A new twist on an old favorite.

2 6-inch pita rounds
6-oz. can tuna, drained
1 T. mayonnaise
1 T. dill pickle relish
1/4 t. dill weed

1/8 t. salt
1/2 tomato, cut into thin
   wedges
1/2 c. shredded Cheddar
   cheese

Arrange pitas on an ungreased baking sheet. Bake at 400 degrees for 5 minutes, or until lightly toasted. Mix together tuna, mayonnaise, relish, dill weed and salt in a small bowl; spread onto pitas. Arrange tomato wedges on top; sprinkle with cheese. Bake for an additional 5 minutes, until cheese melts. Serves 2.

Keep sour cream fresh longer...store the
container upside-down in the fridge.

Comfort Foods for One or Two

Fried Potato Sandwiches

Denise Cooper
Wolverine Lake, MI

My grandmother used to make these sandwiches during the Depression when meat was expensive. They are still a comfort food for my family and me.

1 potato, thinly sliced
2 to 3 t. butter, divided
2 eggs, beaten

4 slices white bread
2 slices American cheese
mayonnaise to taste

In a skillet over medium heat, fry potato slices in half the butter until golden and crispy. Drain on a paper towel. Add remaining butter to skillet and scramble eggs as desired. For each sandwich, arrange half of potato slices on one slice bread; top with half the eggs and one slice cheese. Spread mayonnaise on remaining bread; place over cheese. Makes 2 sandwiches.

Pita Pierogie Pizza

Judy Lange
Imperial, PA

So good and so fast...a tasty meatless meal.

1/2 c. mashed potatoes
1 pita round
1 T. green onion, sliced

1/2 c. shredded Cheddar cheese

Spread potatoes on pita; sprinkle with green onion and cheese. Bake at 350 degrees for 8 to 10 minutes, until heated through. Serves one.

Have your loaf and eat it too! As soon as you bring home bread from the bakery, wrap half in plastic wrap and freeze. It'll keep its fresh-baked taste for 2 to 3 months...just thaw at room temperature.

Summer Squash Casserole

Debi DeVore
Dover, OH

A potluck favorite, scaled down to serve two.

2 yellow squash, sliced
1/4 c. onion, chopped
1/2 t. salt, divided
1 egg, beaten
1/4 c. mayonnaise
2 t. sugar

pepper to taste
1/4 c. shredded Cheddar
  cheese
2 T. corn flake cereal, crushed
1-1/2 t. butter, melted

In a small saucepan, cover squash and onion with water. Add 1/4 teaspoon salt and bring to a boil. Reduce heat and simmer, uncovered, for 2 minutes, until squash is crisp-tender. Drain; set aside. In a bowl, beat egg, mayonnaise, sugar, pepper and remaining salt until well blended. Stir in cheese and squash mixture. Transfer to a greased 2-cup casserole dish. Toss cereal and butter together and sprinkle on top. Bake, uncovered, at 350 degrees for 25 to 30 minutes until golden and bubbly. Serves 2.

Green Beans Deluxe

Shelley Turner
Boise, ID

Why wait until Thanksgiving...the two of you can enjoy these yummy beans anytime.

1/2 c. cream of mushroom
  soup
3 T. milk
1/2 t. soy sauce
1/8 t. pepper

1-1/3 c. frozen green beans,
  thawed
1/2 c. French fried onions,
  divided

Combine soup, milk, soy sauce and pepper in a bowl; stir in green beans and 1/4 cup onions. Transfer to a lightly greased 2-cup baking dish; sprinkle with remaining onions. Bake, uncovered, at 400 degrees for 12 to 15 minutes, until bubbly. Serves 2.

Crispy Bacon Mac & Cheese

Penny Sherman
Cumming, GA

Add a crisp green salad...dinner is served!

6-oz. pkg. macaroni & cheese
   mix
1/4 c. bacon bits
3 T. Italian-style dry bread
   crumbs

1 T. fresh chives, chopped
1 T. butter, melted

Prepare macaroni & cheese as package directs; stir in bacon. Spoon into 2 greased 12-ounce casserole dishes and set aside. In a small bowl, combine bread crumbs, chives and butter. Mix well and sprinkle over each casserole. Bake, uncovered, at 375 degrees for 20 to 25 minutes, until topping is golden. Serves 2.

Almost-homemade tomato soup for two...just the thing for a rainy day! Combine a can of tomato soup with a can of diced tomatoes and simmer until hot. Add a little Italian seasoning plus a bit of cream or milk, if you like it creamy.

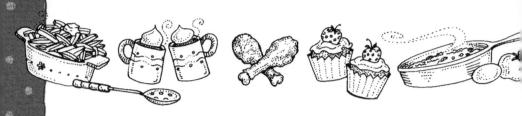

Creamy Chicken & Rice

Geneva Rogers
Gillette, WY

Choose your favorite chicken parts...if you prefer white meat,
slice chicken breasts in half so they'll bake evenly.

3/4 c. instant rice, uncooked
10-3/4 oz. can cream of
   chicken soup

1-1/2 lbs. chicken
2 T. onion soup mix

Mix together rice and soup; spread in an 8"x8" baking dish.
Arrange chicken pieces on top; sprinkle with soup mix. Cover with
aluminum foil; bake at 325 degrees for 1-1/2 hours, until chicken
juices run clear when pierced. Serves 2.

Glazed Lemon Chicken

Kendall Hale
Lynn, MA

It's so easy to vary the flavor of this glaze! Try rosemary
instead of tarragon...use lime juice for the lemon juice.

1-1/2 lbs. chicken
2 T. butter, melted
2 T. lemon juice

1/2 t. dried tarragon
salt and pepper to taste

Arrange chicken pieces skin-side down on a broiler pan; set
aside. Mix butter, lemon juice and tarragon in a small bowl.
Brush mixture over chicken; add salt and pepper to taste. Broil
for 15 minutes, until lightly browned. Turn chicken over; brush
with remaining mixture and broil an additional 10 to 15 minutes,
until chicken juices run clear when pierced. Serves 2.

Add a zesty marinade to plastic zipping bags of
uncooked chicken and freeze. The chicken will be
deliciously seasoned when you thaw it for cooking.

Spaghetti Red

Joyrene Kitsmiller
Wichita, KS

*My father fixed this for supper whenever Mother had to be away.
He served it with a shaker of chili powder, grated Parmesan
cheese and buttered toast...a cozy little supper for the two of us.*

1/4 lb. ground beef
dried, minced onion and
    seasoning salt to taste

14-3/4 oz. can spaghetti in
    tomato sauce with cheese

Brown ground beef, onion and seasoning salt in a non-stick
skillet over medium-high heat; drain. Stir in canned spaghetti.
Mix together until heated through. Makes 2 servings.

If Mom's tried & true meatloaf recipe is too large for
your small family, make meatloaf muffins instead! Fill
greased muffin cups and bake for 20 to 25 minutes at
350 degrees. Enjoy some now...freeze the rest for later.

Cube Steaks Stroganoff

Tori Willis
Champaign, IL

Serve over cooked egg noodles or rice.

2 T. all-purpose flour
1 T. dried parsley, divided
1/4 t. pepper
2 4-oz. beef cube steaks

1/2 c. onion, thinly sliced
2-1/2 oz. jar sliced mushrooms
3 T. sour cream
1 T. milk

Combine flour, one teaspoon parsley and pepper in a shallow dish; coat steaks in mixture. Spray a skillet with butter-flavored non-stick vegetable spray; sauté steaks over medium heat for 4 minutes on each side. Add onion, mushrooms and liquid from mushrooms. Lower heat; cover and simmer for 12 to 15 minutes, until onion is tender. Place steaks on 2 dinner plates; cover to keep warm. Stir sour cream, milk and remaining parsley into pan juices in skillet; cook and stir until warmed through. Spoon sour cream mixture onto steaks. Serves 2.

Steak Diane

Vickie

Add some tiny new potatoes and steamed asparagus...delicious!

1 clove garlic, sliced
2 T. butter
2 beef ribeye steaks
1/4 t. salt

1/8 t. pepper
1 T. fresh parsley, minced
1 T. fresh chives, minced
1-1/2 t. Worcestershire sauce

In a skillet over medium-low heat, sauté garlic in butter until tender. Remove garlic with a slotted spoon; discard. Add steaks and lightly brown to desired doneness, about 3 to 4 minutes per side. Remove steaks to 2 dinner plates; sprinkle with salt and pepper. Add parsley, chives and Worcestershire sauce to pan juices; stir and heat through. Drizzle pan juices over steaks. Serves 2.

Pan-Fried Pork Chops

Annette Ingram
Grand Rapids, MI

My son always requests these chops for his birthday dinner.

1/2 c. all-purpose flour
1 t. seasoned salt
1/8 t. pepper
4 center-cut pork chops
1 egg, beaten

2 T. milk
1/2 c. dry bread crumbs
2 T. shortening
1/4 c. chicken broth

Mix together flour, salt and pepper; coat pork chops in mixture and set aside. Whisk together egg and milk; dip chops into egg mixture, then into bread crumbs. Heat shortening in a skillet over medium heat. Add chops and cook for 3 minutes on each side until golden. Add broth; lower heat, cover and simmer about 45 minutes, or until tender. Uncover for last 5 minutes of cooking time. Serves 2.

Topped with gravy, chili or just creamy butter,
baked potatoes are a meal in themselves! Cut
baking time in half...microwave potatoes on
high for 4 minutes on each side, then bake
at 450 degrees for 20 minutes, until tender.

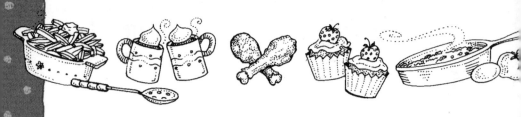

Bread Pudding

Marlene Darnell
Newport Beach, CA

Wonderful made with a leftover cinnamon roll too.

1 slice bread, cubed	3 T. water
2 T. raisins	2 T. sugar
1 egg	1/4 t. cinnamon
1/2 c. evaporated milk	1/4 t. nutmeg

Divide bread and raisins between 2 greased one-cup baking dishes; set aside. Blend together egg, milk and water; pour over bread mixture and set aside. Mix sugar and spices; sprinkle over top. Bake, uncovered, at 350 degrees for 30 to 35 minutes, or until a knife inserted near center comes out clean. Serve warm. Serves 2.

Rose's Baked Custard

Rose Jones
Champaign, IL

A simple dessert like Grandma used to make.

1 egg	3/4 t. vanilla extract
1 c. milk	1/8 t. salt
3 T. sugar	1/8 t. nutmeg

Beat egg in a small bowl; stir in milk, sugar, vanilla and salt. Pour into 2 ungreased 6-ounce custard cups. Sprinkle with nutmeg. Set custard cups in a baking pan filled with 1/2 inch of hot water. Bake at 350 degrees for 35 minutes, until set. Serves 2.

Delectable fruit like peaches needn't go to waste if it ripens quicker than you can eat it. Purée it, freeze and use later for topping cheesecake or waffles.